Youth & Youth Work in Ireland

*This book is dedicated to the memory of
Kathleen Ryan who died on 8th June 2011.*

YOUTH & YOUTH WORK IN IRELAND

Caroline Coyne & Josephine Donohoe

Gill & Macmillan

Gill & Macmillan
Hume Avenue
Park West
Dublin 12
with associated companies throughout the world
www.gillmacmillan.ie

© Caroline Coyne & Josephine Donohoe 2013

978 07171 5635 1

Index compiled by Adam Pozner
Illustrations by Rosa Devine
Print origination by Carole Lynch
Printed by GraphyCems, Spain

A CIP catalogue record is available for this book
from the British Library

Contents

Acknowledgements

We wish to thank our families and friends who provided continuous encouragement and support, not to mention technical support, peer reviews and endless cups of tea.

We would like to particularly express our appreciation to Youth Work Ireland for access to their library.

CC & JD

Introduction

We wrote this book because of the difficulties that we as teachers had in accessing suitable material for our youth work students. Of course there is a wealth of information available online, from the youth work libraries and information centres; the problem is not that information is not out there, but that it did not exist in one accessible textbook. This book brings together for the first time material on youth and youth work with a specifically Irish focus aimed primarily at FETAC Level 5. It would also be useful as a basic reference at other levels of education and for youth work services for volunteers and trainees alike.

A practical rather than a theoretical approach is taken in the presentation of the material. Activities, tasks, 'think abouts' and scenarios are interspersed at relevant stages throughout the text and are designed to provoke thinking, learning and discussion as appropriate. Furthermore, some of the activities are designed to be used as assignments and projects, while others may be adapted for use in youth work services.

The material presented here is more than sufficient for the study of the mandatory components in the Youth Work programme at FETAC Level 5. In addition, resources are signposted at the end of each section so that the learner who wishes to explore further can do so in a structured fashion. These resources are not exhaustive but are readily accessible on the Internet, in libraries and bookshops. It should also be noted that although numerous website addresses are given, they do change over time, but can usually be found under archived material. The role of the youth worker is covered in a general way in Section 2, and there is a focus throughout the book on the role of the youth worker or implications for the youth service as relevant to specific areas.

There are a few sections that go beyond the requirements of the Level 5 programmes. One is the section on child protection, which is covered in considerable detail as it is essential that all those involved with children and young people be knowledgeable and confident in this area. Another is that of equality and diversity. All of the material presented is underpinned by a commitment to principles of equality, which we believe should be intrinsic to all youth work. In this section in particular, the learner is required to be 'active' in their own learning. We also include a small section on peer education, as this approach is pivotal to empowering young people and in youth work practice.

Finally, in writing this book we are bringing together in one place information that will be useful and relevant for all those interested in youth work and as a sound starting point for further studies.

1

Young People and Society

Adolescence and the Theories of Adolescence

Young People in Families and Family Law

Education

Employment

Youth and Justice

Youth Culture, Subculture and Globalisation

This section aims to give a broad overview of the main factors influencing young people's lives in Ireland today. A basic understanding of the period of adolescence is of course essential, but every adolescent grows up in the context of different family, community, social frameworks and cultural influences. A number of these contexts are identified, defined, explored and explained to a degree that will enable the learner to explore these areas in greater depth and to explore other areas not covered here. Descriptions and details of legislation and services are given in the understanding that these are constantly changing, but the resources and guidance provided should facilitate the update of facts and figures.

Adolescence and the Theories of Adolescence

An understanding of the phase of human growth and development known as adolescence is crucial to an examination of the development of youth work approaches and youth services. The purpose of this chapter is to outline basic facts, core theories and relevant issues in relation to puberty and adolescence. Ideas relating to adolescence and adolescent development change over time and across cultures, and these considerations will also be examined. Finally the chapter provides a bibliography to outline further material for a comprehensive and in-depth study of the area.

The meaning of adolescence

According to the World Health Organisation, the period of adolescence occurs during the second decade of a person's life (10–20 years) and can be defined as the transitional stage during which a juvenile matures into an adult. This transition involves biological, social and psychological changes.

The term 'teenager' is often used in Irish society as synonymous with adolescence, but in fact, the term refers to young people between the ages of thirteen and nineteen years. The terms *tweenie* or *pre-teen* have appeared in recent times and refer to the pre-adolescent period from eight or nine up to twelve years. It seems that the terms *teenager* and *tweenie* have appeared primarily in the western world initially in the domains of marketing and advertising.

Physical development

Sexual maturation: The pattern of physical development in adolescence appears to be fairly consistent but individual development varies. The term 'puberty' is commonly used when referring to physical development. Growth spurts are generally the most obvious sign that puberty has begun, but many changes will have happened prior to this.

The word 'menarche' refers to the onset of menstruation. In contemporary Western society menarche occurs for 95% of girls between the ages of 12 and 15 years. Typically the first steps of puberty will have begun two years prior to this. The age of onset of menstruation is influenced by diet and health. In 1840 the average age was 17 years whereas today it is usually 12–13 years. Periods may be irregular for a time and fertility delayed after starting menstruation but it is possible to become pregnant immediately. It is this irregularity that probably gives rise to the commonly-held belief that younger adolescent girls may not become pregnant easily.

Table 1.1.1 Indicators of adolescent sexual maturation

Girls	Boys
Initial growth spurt	Scrotum darkens and testes descend
Breast development	Appearance of pubic hair
Appearance of pubic hair	Penis enlarges
Appearance of underarm and body hair	Growth spurt
Vaginal discharge	Ejaculation
Development of underarm sweat glands	Appearance of underarm and body hair
Menstruation	Appearance of facial hair
	Development of underarm sweat glands
	Deepening of voice and appearance of Adam's apple

Spermarche is the boys' equivalent of menarche, namely when they first ejaculate and become capable of reproduction. The average age of fertility for boys in the Western world is thought to be somewhere in the region of 12–14 years. The outward signs of puberty such as beard growth and voice deepening occurs quite late in the sequence of sexual development.

Behind all these changes is an influx of hormones and the following table broadly outlines the relationship between hormones and development.

Table 1.1.2 Major hormones that contribute to physical growth and development

Gland	Hormone	Aspects of Growth
Thyroid	Thyroxine	Brain development and rate of growth
Adrenal	Adrenal androgen	Development of secondary sex characteristics in girls such as growth spurts and pubic hair
Testes (boys)	Testosterone	Triggers sequence of changes in sex characteristics in boys
Ovaries (girls)	Oestrogen (estradiol)	Development of menstrual cycle and breasts
Pituitary	General growth hormone	Rate of growth and signals other glands

The skeleton: Adolescents may grow 3–6 inches over a number of years. Most girls grow until approximately 16 years; boys continue to grow until 18 years. Some development is uneven (hands and feet grow first, followed by arms and legs) so adolescents may appear gangly and out of proportion. Facial bones also change, with the jaws moving forward and forehead becoming more prominent, resulting in a bony, angular appearance.

Girls continue to develop ahead of boys in the area of fine motor development and joint development; boys do not catch up until they are around 18 years old.

Muscular system: Both boys and girls become stronger as their muscles become denser and thicker, but boys grow much stronger.

In adult men, about 40% of total body mass is muscle and the percentage of fat drops to about 14%.

In adult women, about 24% of body mass is constituted by muscle and fat rises to about 24%.

Heart and lungs: Both increase in size during these years, and the heart rate drops. Changes in both are more marked in boys.

A decrease in body fat, an increase in muscle mass and a lower heart rate all facilitate greater endurance and strength in boys as compared to girls.

Cognitive development and the brain

Growth occurs in parts of the brain that control spatial perception and motor function between the ages of 13 and 15 years and again around the age of 17; at these times more energy is also produced and used in the brain.

The brain also develops in ways that enable young people to think in increasingly abstract terms, allowing for philosophical thought and inventiveness, for example.

Another growth spurt occurs around 17 years, which may facilitate the development of logic and planning functions.

Younger adolescents differ from both children and older adolescents in terms of their brain abilities. As a result, their approaches to life and problem-solving also differ.

As the child develops into an adult, the growth of the brain facilitates a major shift in the young person's ability to think, marking a change from concrete to abstract thought. Abstract thought is based on general concepts and ideas, and not on any particular real person, thing or situation.

- adolescents can think about things that are possible but not observable
- adolescents can plan ahead

- adolescents can think through theories and hypotheses and test them out in their head
- adolescents can think about their own thought processes – this is called metacognition.

Social and emotional development

> Social development includes the forming of relationships, interacting with others, the development of a sense of identity and development of life skills

> Emotional development includes the expression of feelings and the development of attachment, self-esteem, self-confidence, autonomy and responsibility

The expectations that the young person has of themselves along with the expectations that people around them have of them are very important for psychological adjustment in adolescence. These expectations are definitely influenced by the society and culture in which the young person is growing up. In short, adolescence begins in biology but ends in culture. What is culture? Culture is a set of beliefs, customs and patterns of behaviour that are distinctive to a particular group. Your status as an adolescent, child, woman and man is defined by the society in which you live and the period in history during which you live.

In some cultures the stage of development of adolescence is not recognised at all. In such cultures, a child becomes an adult when they have acquired the knowledge and skills to ensure their survival and that of their dependents.

Think about...

...the life of a 14-year-old girl in California in comparison to a 14-year-old in the Masai tribe in Kenya. The first is at school, dancing, dating, playing games, but primarily her responsibility is to engage in studying to enable her to get a job and support herself financially in maybe ten years' time. The girl in Kenya has a child and is working within her husband's family under the eye of her mother-in-law, her status equal to other young women in her tribe.

 **Activity:**

Find out about the lives and experiences of adolescents in other cultures. Find out about various rites of passage.

The transition to adulthood is marked in most societies, in some more clearly than others. There are innumerable formal *rites of passage* such as endurance tests, trance dancing, killing your first large animal or religious rites such as confirmation and bar mitzvah. In many cultures roles and expectations are clearly marked out for the young person.

No single common rite or clear expectation exists across all Western societies. Entering secondary school, getting a job, getting a driver's license, voting rights and doing military service are all markers in one way or another. But if a group of young people in Ireland was asked when they would consider themselves to have become adults, you would get a variety of answers.

The transition to adulthood is ambiguous, so it could be said that many of our young people live in a sort of limbo. Peer pressure is often (although not always) viewed as negative in our society, but in others it tends to be viewed as positive, giving courage and strength to the young person to go through with a particular task or rite of passage.

Because of cognitive changes and the ability to think increasingly in the abstract, the young person's self concept becomes much more complex. Whereas the younger child will focus more on the physical and quantifiable, e.g. 'I came first in the race, so I am a good athlete', the adolescent will focus on more abstract or ideological traits about humanness, beliefs, psychological characteristics, morals and values, e.g. 'Why is it so important to win a race anyway?'

They will even begin to think about thinking itself!

Understandably, self-concepts predict behaviour: if a young person thinks they are good at something, they will persevere with it; if a young person sees themselves as unlovable, they will be less likely to persevere with relationships; young people from relatively happy and stable family backgrounds seem to form longer-lasting relationships at a younger age. Obviously, lots of other variables are at play also.

Girls seem to be more objective about what they are good at and how they compare with others than boys, who seem to attend more to internal, self-defined standards. Perhaps this is a cultural influence.

Theories of adolescent development

Erik Erikson (1902–1994): Psychosocial Theory

Erikson posits a stage model of human growth and development of which adolescence is the fifth stage. According to Erikson, the central crisis in adolescence is 'identity versus role confusion'. The child's sense of identity (reached through earlier stages of secure attachment and sense of autonomy) becomes challenged amid physical growth, hormonal changes and a growing awareness of future adult roles and responsibilities. A new identity must be formed so that the individual can adapt to their various adult roles, including occupational, sexual, social, religious and other roles. At this point the individual enters what Erikson calls a 'psychological moratorium'. Basically, the person in adolescence goes through a period when they explore and test out various ideas, beliefs and goals. Some of these will directly contradict those of their parents, and at this stage the peer group becomes an important source of support and new ideas. The peer group can give a sense of security and become to some extent be the young person's buffer against emotional distress, but in the end, each adolescent must achieve an integrated self with his own pattern of beliefs, occupational goals and relationships. Adolescents who do not successfully negotiate a mature adult identity suffer what Erikson terms 'identity confusion'. Identity confusion occurs when the young person is unable to negotiate a clear identity for themselves from the profusion of choices available.

David Elkind (1931–): Theory of Adolescent Egocentrism

David Elkind introduced the concepts of adolescent egocentrism, imaginary audience and personal fable.

Adolescent egocentrism refers to the heightened self-consciousness and self-absorption that is characteristic of the young adolescent. The term 'imaginary audience' seeks to describe the phenomenon whereby adolescents believe that all eyes are on them, all comments are about them and everyone is interested in them, whether the attention is positive or negative. A young person tends to care deeply about what this imaginary audience thinks of them. The 'personal fable' is a name for the adolescent belief that 'it won't happen to me' and can help to explain irrational and risk-taking behaviours; it can also help to explain the belief that 'no one understands me'.

Lawrence Kohlberg (1927–1987): Theory of Moral Development
Lawrence Kohlberg focussed on the moral development of the adolescent, and his theory posits three broad stages: preconventional, conventional and postconventional.

The early adolescent may have a heightened sense of fairness and sharing (preconventional reasoning). On reaching the conventional reasoning stage, the young person is now paying more attention to wider issues and is not just concerned with feeling good personally. Characteristic of this stage is a respect for authority and a belief in doing one's duty. Postconventional moral reasoning is concerned with broad moral perspectives and universal principles, with which the person is able to consider conflicting perspectives and different standpoints and make judgements based on them. For example, human life is sacred and the taking of life is wrong, but there are times when this is not so clear cut such as when considering euthanasia or fighting to defend one's community in wartime. Relationships are very influential in moral reasoning. A sense of fairness and responding to someone in need are also influential.

Anti-social behaviour and moral reasoning:
Prosocial behaviour co-relates to higher moral reasoning and anti-social behaviour to the lowest levels of moral reasoning.

Young people who engage in anti-social behaviours are thought to have immature moral reasoning. They have difficulty seeing a situation from someone else's perspective. Obviously, family and social issues are huge influential factors here. Those with the most disturbing patterns of delinquency have exhibited worrying behaviour much earlier in their lives, usually as a result of their own stressful and complex experiences. Efforts to influence their behaviour must focus on a variety of social and emotional contexts.

James E. Marcia (1902–): Psychosocial Development

Marcia's Theory of Identity Achievement is based on Erikson's ideas. He suggests that adolescence has two key parts:

- Crisis
- Commitment

Four identity statuses are possible:

- *Identity diffusion*: no crisis, no commitment. At this stage the individual is just not interested in exploring alternatives. This is primarily associated with the younger adolescent who continues to accept parental values, beliefs and guidance.
- *Foreclosure*: the person accepts parentally or culturally defined commitment without crisis. This is characteristic of a young adult who accepts their parent's choices for them unquestioningly.
- *Moratorium*: crisis is ongoing and no commitment has been made; typical of many contemporary Western middle-class young people.
- *Identity achievement*: crisis is over and person has committed to an identity. Life choices have been made about career, religion, marriage, etc.

According to Marcia, to achieve a fully mature identity the young person must have examined his/her values and goals and have reached a firm commitment.

Jean Piaget (1896–1980): Cognitive Stage Theory of Development

Piaget focuses on the intellectual processes that occur in developmental stages; these include *Sensorimotor, Preoperational, Concrete Operational* and *Formal Operational*.

Generally speaking, the young adolescent is moving through the Formal Operational stage, which begins around the age of eleven years. During this stage thought becomes more abstract, incorporating the principles of formal logic. Thinking becomes less tied to concrete reality. Formal Operational thought can be abstract, idealistic and logical.

Abstract thinking is probably easiest understood by comparing it to concrete thinking. A concrete thinker will look at a picture of the Statue of Liberty and see a statue of a woman with a torch in her hand; an abstract thinker may think of freedom and justice. Formal operational thought is also logical or as Piaget called it 'hyper-deductive reasoning' when a young person begins to work things out systematically and scientifically. The development of abstract thinking allows an adolescent to begin to think about their own thoughts and to become idealistic, i.e. to develop metacognitive understanding.

Urie Bronfebrenner (1917–2005): The Ecological Systems Theory

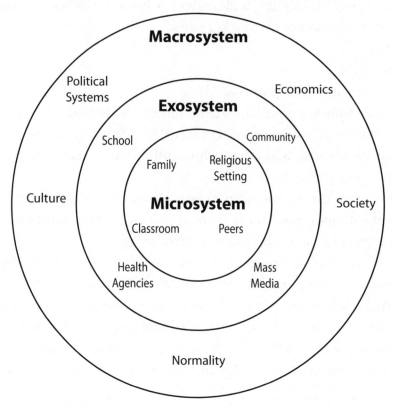

This is an ecological, holistic model that looks at adolescence in the context in which the adolescent lives. The Ecological Systems Theory states that the world in which adolescents live has a huge impact on young people and vice versa. They are influenced by

- the times that they live in (chronosystem);
- the general social, economic, political and cultural aspects of the society in which they live (macrosystem)
- the wider community, mass media, government agencies, church (exosystem)
- the family, school religion, friends (microsystems)
- and finally, by the relationship between two or more of these systems (mesosystem)

Scenario:

A group of young people attending a youth service has an assignment due for assessment as part of a FETAC course. The teacher does not give out the next assignment until the current one is completed.

Sam and Joseph have worked steadily through the last few weeks and have their assignment ready for submission.

Joanne has a part-time job and was called into work to cover for someone who is ill, so she did not finish the assignment.

Sarah and Stephen always leave things until the last minute, but this time, despite staying up all night, the assignment is not ready. Another two days will do it!

Cliona knew Joanne wouldn't be finished, so, hoping for an assignment extension, she went to a party on Saturday that lasted until well into Sunday morning. She has not finished either.

There is a dilemma: if the teacher gives an extension, then there will be less time to get the next assignment covered. However, if those who have not finished the work are not allowed to submit, then they will fail the module and will not get their certificate at the end of the year. What might be a fair solution? Would adolescents at different stages come up with different solutions?

Gender identity

Sex Role Identity: refers to gender-related aspects of the psychological self. This is seen as a continuum as opposed to distinctly female- or male-related. Thus a female can have masculine characteristics and vice versa.

Four basic sex role types:
- Masculine – traditional masculine traits include toughness, competitiveness, independence.
- Feminine – traditional feminine traits include caring and compliance.
- Androgynous – both masculine and feminine traits.
- Undifferentiated – lack of any identifiable masculine or feminine traits.

Ethnic identity

Ethnic identity means identification as a member of a specific ethnic group, commitment to that group, its values and its attitudes. It can be difficult to maintain an ethnic identity when the majority of a population belongs to a different ethnic group. If, as someone with a minority ethnic identity, you attempt to join the majority group you may be ostracised by your own, smaller group; if you stick with your ethnic group, your choices may be limited. Studies suggest that Western culture values individual achievement and the individual more than some other cultures where community and commitment to the family is given high status. Thus minority ethnic adolescents growing up in a 'traditional' household with Western cultural values may indeed find life very hard and confusing. This is very relevant in contemporary Ireland for young people who are first- or second-generation immigrants but whose upbringing and family values are more 'traditional'.

Think about…:

The following young people, who are in the same club: Rachel, who is the oldest; Jennifer, whose family is experiencing financial hardship; Derek, who is hard working; and Omar, who is a very skilled football player. One afternoon they thought it would be a good idea to play football with some of the younger club members. Rachel helped for 2 hours, as did Jennifer and Omar. Derek helped to set up the matches and cleaned up afterwards, and so worked for nearly 4 hours in total. At the end, the group leader gave them €20 and they had to decide how to divide it up. The young people's decision as to which way to divide the money could be influenced by their personal, family or community beliefs and traditions. The decision could be based on three different ideological approaches:

- **Need-based** – Jennifer would get the most (This would be characteristic of a social welfare approach.)
- **According to effort** – Derek worked the longest and hardest, so he gets the most. (This would be characteristic of a labour-based approach.)
- **Collectivist** – all four get the same amount because they all helped, and because without any one of them the activity would not have gone ahead. (This would be based on equality and community need.)

Thinking about this situation should help a youth worker to understand how young people from different backgrounds or cultures may have different thoughts on fairness and justice and to appreciate that all young people in a group regardless of culture may have differing expectations and views.

How do you think the money should be divided, and why?

Social relationships in adolescence

Relationships with parents:
Conflict between parents and adolescents is recognised and has been well researched. More worryingly, conflict appears to be generally expected, yet one researcher in the US found that it only causes major disruption in the parent–child relationship in about 5–10% of families. The conflict arises principally from the primary goal of adolescence, to strive for independence within the confines of close familial relationships.

Attachment:
Across a variety of cultures and social groups, research has shown that the majority of people come through adolescence with a strong attachment to their parents, although this sense of attachment does seem to dip at around 15 or 16 years.

A strong bond with parents in early childhood seems to be a good indicator of how things will go in adolescence. Parenting styles and family structures also affect the relationship between adolescents and their parents.

Peer relationships:
Loyalty, faithfulness and intimacy become very important during the adolescent period. Friendships last longer than they did in childhood in part because adolescents work harder at conflict resolution. Maintaining friendships and continuing in activities appear to be linked to and contribute to stability in friendships. It is suggested that girls seem to prefer other girls with the same level of romantic attachments, whereas boys' preferences tend to be linked to activities or athletic achievement. It is not surprising, therefore, that girls seem to spend less time with their girlfriends when they have a boyfriend than the opposite.

Peer groups:
Peer group attachment and involvement is at its most potent around the ages of 13 or 14, during which time conformity to the group identity peaks while self-esteem dips slightly. As self-identity grows stronger, the peer group, though stable, may have less influence.

Thus while Erikson and Marcia are right in asserting that the peer group has a major influence, that influence is neither all powerful nor all negative.

Peer group structure:

The main structures of adolescent peer groups have been identified as *cliques, crowds* and *couples.* Cliques tend to predominate in early adolescence and tend to be same-sex; they may also have identifiable shared characteristics or interests. Crowds are mixed-gender and are label-based – think nerds, sporty types, Goths, etc. By Leaving Certificate age, crowds became less important than significant friends and couples.

Romantic relationships:

The shift from same-sex friendships to romantic relationships is fairly gradual but more rapid with girls. Although sex drive is a force, social and cultural factors are just as important. Again, relationships with parents and earlier friendships do seem to signpost the ease with which an adolescent moves into romantic relationships.

Intimacy, communication and reading social cues are just as important at this stage as physical sexuality. Engagement in sexual acts depends on a lot of variables including the stability of the family background, sense of security, religion and culture. According to Santrock (2010) early dating and sexual activity appear to be more common among the disadvantaged of every ethnic group.

For the vast majority of young people, their pathway through adolescence includes a progression in peer relationships from same-sex cliques to mixed-sex groups to heterosexual dating pairs. Yet for a significant proportion of young people, their sexual orientation will be lesbian, gay, bisexual or transgender (LGBT). Studies of prenatal hormonal patterns suggest that sexual orientation is programmed before birth, but these studies do not rule out the influence of environmental factors.

Many LGBT adolescents face a high level of stress due to ridicule, prejudice and discrimination. See 'LGBT Adolescents' on page 17 for a more in-depth analysis.

All of the theories, research and studies clearly indicate that how any one person matures through adolescence into adulthood depends on a combination of factors. Any one theory or study does not tell the whole story, but background research and knowledge should enable the youth worker to be both more understanding and to offer more appropriate support.

Adolescent health

Adolescence is the healthiest, heartiest period of life, when, other things being equal, the individual is at their healthiest, fittest, strongest and most fertile. That said, there are health issues specific to adolescence, for example mental health problems and eating disorders (see p. 16). Other issues, though not generally age-dependant, are of particular concern to adolescents, such as sexual activity, drugs and alcohol. Culture, religion and ethnicity are significant factors in considering these concerns, keeping in mind that across all societies and cultural groups, those who most abuse substances and/or are most sexually active come from disadvantaged groups or have experienced significant problems earlier in life.

Psychosomatic symptoms are more prevalent in adolescents than in adults, and generally appear in response to stresses or perceived stresses. Risky behaviours and risk-taking can be associated with need for acceptance by peer group or showing independence; it also fits with Elkind's theory of the personal fable. Sensation-seeking is heightened and accounts for an increase in accidents in this age group.

Sex, violence, drugs and alcohol are big issues in terms of this desire for new, heightened experiences. The media tend to portray sex, violence and substance use, but not their consequences.

Sexual behaviour:

Social factors and moral beliefs are hugely important to sexual behaviour and related risks. Boys are found consistently to be more sexually active than girls. Risk-taking is evident here, as adolescents are less likely to use contraception or protection. The younger they are, the less likely they are to use either. Research indicates that alcohol abuse is associated with over a quarter of adolescent sexual encounters. (Santrock, 2010)

Teenage pregnancy:

Social class, advantage and disadvantage are inversely related to teenage pregnancy, i.e. the more disadvantaged young people are, the more likely they are to be at risk. Still, relatively few girls under 15 years of age get pregnant in Ireland. See section on Demography, p. 25. On the whole, teenage pregnancy has increased enormously in the last 50 years because of socio-cultural factors, but in the UK and US it has actually fallen. Pregnancies have increased among older adolescents. Across all ethnic groups, less than one fifth of young adolescent parents maintain their original relationship one year after the birth.

Peer and parental rejection, early sexual activity and high unemployment all increase likelihood of a young adolescents conceiving.

On the other hand, doing well at school and having a goal has the opposite effect. So providing purpose, formulating goals and increasing self-esteem and confidence is helpful in preventing pregnancies – not forgetting, of course, sex education.

Substance abuse:

Sensation-seeking, a characteristic of the adolescent, is a factor in drug and alcohol abuse. In Ireland, recent research indicates that heavy and binge drinking has increased enormously among young adolescents. Alcohol poisoning and liver damage is a risk for all, particularly for girls who overindulge, because the female body is less able than that of males to process the toxins.

Tobacco use seems to be less to do with sensation-seeking and more with peer influence. Research shows that even young people who are very aware of the effects may still take up smoking. Parents seem to have the most influence over whether children will take up a smoking habit.

Eating disorders indicate significant mental health problems. See Section 4 for more on health and well-being.

■ Bulimia – binge eating followed by induced vomiting. The individual tends to be obsessed by their weight, and it is nearly always girls who present with bulimia. Bulimia is unheard of in places where food is scarce. Consequences include tooth decay, stomach irritation, lowered body temperature, chemical disturbances, hormonal imbalances and loss of hair.

■ Anorexia nervosa – extreme dieting, excessive exercising, fear of gaining weight and vomiting. Again, mostly prevalent in girls and young women. Consequences are very serious and consistent with starvation: sleep disturbance, cessation of menstruation, insensitivity to pain, loss of hair, cardiovascular problems and low blood pressure are just some of the potential effects. Some sufferers die from starvation or complications of the above symptoms.

Self-harm, suicide, sexual health and substance misuse is covered in more detail in Section 4.

As stated at the beginning, the purpose of this chapter is to furnish broad outlines and basic information about the period of adolescence. More in-depth study should be undertaken, and the following are recommended resources. Much of the information in this chapter was gleaned from these sources.

References, resources and further reading

Beckett, Chris, 2002, *Human Growth and Development*, London: Sage

Boyd, B. and H. L. Bee, 2011, *Lifespan Development* (6th ed.), Boston: Allyn and Bacon

Gardiner, H. W. and C. Kosmitzki, 2010, *Lives Across Cultures*, Boston: Allyn and Bacon

Lalor, K., De Roiste, Á. and Maurice Devlin, 2007, *Young People in Contemporary Ireland*, Dublin: Gill and Macmillan.

Santrock, J. W., 2010, *Lifespan Development* (13th ed.), New York: McGraw-Hill.

Santrock, J. W., 2011, *Adolescence* (14th ed.), New York: McGraw-Hill.

LGBT adolescents

LGBT stands for lesbian, gay, bisexual and transgender. *Homosexual* is now considered a bit outdated, as it was originally a medical term to refer to, mainly, men who were attracted to other men.

- Lesbian – a woman who is attracted to other women
- Gay – can refer to men attracted to men or women attracted to women. Currently the term 'gay' can also be used as a term of abuse and as a means of homophobic bullying.
- Bisexual – refers to men or women who are attracted to both sexes
- Transgender – refers to people who do not feel that their biological sex matches their gender identity. The term is used to describe a wide variety of different gender identities and gender presentations.
- Transsexual – refers to person who is living or desires to live as a gender other than the one they were born into.
- Transvestite – refers to a person who sometimes dresses in clothes considered more appropriate to another gender; a transvestite may be gay, transgender or heterosexual.
- Heterosexual – a person who is attracted to people of the opposite sex.
- Heterosexist – the assumption that heterosexuality is better and/or more natural than other sexual orientations. The assumption that everyone around you is heterosexual is a form of heterosexism.
- Sexual orientation – the emotional, romantic and/or sexual attraction to persons of a particular sex.

- ■ Sexual identity – refers to whether we consider ourselves to be lesbian, gay, bisexual or transgender.
- ■ Coming out – refers to the decision to tell others of your sexual orientation, which begins with an acceptance of one's own sexual orientation, sometimes referred to as 'coming out' to oneself.
- ■ Homophobia – a fear or hatred of someone who is or seen to be lesbian or gay. Related terms are *biphobia, transphobia.*

The adolescent years are challenging years for all young people; it is a time when they are seeking to develop their identities, what they will become as adults and where they fit into family, community and society. They are also going through puberty, which brings enormous physical, psychological and emotional changes. For many young LGBT people this can be a very difficult time in their lives, and for some, will mean that they feel that they cannot be true to their identity.

Maycock et al. (2009) undertook a comprehensive study of young LGBT people and their lives in Ireland. Key findings were as follows:

- The age when most LGBT people discover their sexual orientation is 12.
- The average age when young, vulnerable LGBT people first self-harm is 16.
- The age when many young people begin to come out to others is 17; the average age is 21.
- This means that most LBGT young people conceal their identity for five years or more throughout their adolescence, which as stated above is the most challenging and critical period of development for all young people.

Young people found the prospect of coming out and coming out itself particularly stressful because of

- Fear of rejection
- Fear of isolation
- Fear of harassment and victimisation

Such fears are often confirmed for the LBGT young person when they come out and subsequently experience discrimination, homophobic bullying and social exclusion, all of which has serious implications for their mental health.

The 2009 report documents the school and day-to-day experiences of LGBT young people.

In school,

- over 50% had been called abusive names by fellow students.
- 34% reported homophobic comments by teachers.
- 20% missed or skipped school because they felt threatened or fearful.

In day-to-day life,

- 80% had been verbally abused.
- 40% had been threatened with violence.
- 25% had been punched, kicked or beaten.
- 10% missed work because they felt threatened or fearful.

Key findings in relation to LGBT people's mental health:

- 27% had self-harmed
- 18% had attempted suicide
- Over 33% under 25 years of age had seriously thought of ending their lives

On the positive side, the report demonstrates that it is the fear, threats and isolation that give rise to the mental problems among the LGBT community, and that those who had support, felt included and enjoyed positive reactions to their sexuality experienced less stress. Hence it can be concluded that being LGBT in itself is not stressful, but rather, real or perceived negative reactions and lack of social support caused stress.

Think about...

...all the terms you have heard used in reference to LGBT people: the good, the bad and the just plain ugly.

...all the terms you have heard used to refer to heterosexual or straight people.

...which list is the longest?

Break down the terms into those that convey positive or negative messages.

Straight Questionnaire

1 What do you think caused you to be straight?
2 When and how did you decide that you were straight?
3 Is it possible that being straight is just a phase that you are going through?
4 If you have never slept with a person of the same sex, how do you know that you're straight?
5 Who have you told that you were straight? How did they react?
6 A disproportionate number of child abusers and molesters are straight. Do you consider it safe to expose children to straight teachers and youth workers?
7 Why do straight people feel they have to persuade or seduce others into joining their lifestyle?
8 Why do straight people place so much emphasis on sex?
9 Do your parents know you are straight?
10 Is it possible being straight stems from a neurotic fear of others of the same sex?

The above was adapted from a questionnaire devised in 1972 by Dr Martin Rochlin, a gay mental health professional and the creator of the Society for the Psychological Study of Lesbian and Gay Issues, part of the American Psychological Association. A full copy of all questions included on the questionnaire can be obtained at *www.lgbt youthnorthwest.org.uk/.../straight_questionnaire* (accessed 4 June 2012)

Clearly, these are examples of questions that LGBT people face all the time about their sexual orientation or gender identity. Did answering any or all of the questions above challenge any of your own ideas about sexual orientation or gender identity?

Consider that 'coming out' refers to the decision to let others know of one's sexual orientation, but only LGBT people have to! As explained below, it can be a particularly stressful time, one when support and affirmation can have a particularly positive effect.

'[Coming out] was a long process and something I still have to do on a regular basis… The whole idea of coming out seemed to dominate my thoughts at that stage. I was always stressing about how to tell people, who to tell and when to do it. I dreaded having to say the words "I am gay".'

'It's hard to pick a moment when you "came out" as it's something that you will have to do to different people at different times throughout your life… I thought I was out to everybody and could leave all that stuff behind. In the last year, I found this to be not quite true. There will always be new people in your life who find out or need to be told or old people in your life you somehow missed.'

Or

'It took me seven years from the time I realised that I wasn't really into girls before I could actually work up the courage to do anything about it.'

'I guess I have always known that I was gay… towards the end of secondary school I realised I had feelings for a girl in my class, and that terrified me, so I jumped back into the closet for another couple of years, never admitting it to myself or others. Then I told myself I was bisexual; that seemed better to me as I would just marry a man and no one would ever know.'

'When my parents asked me I just vomited into the nearest bin. I was so terrified. I cried a lot, I shook from head to toe…'

These are real life extracts taken from 'Coming Out – A Resource Guide and Testimonial' put together by the USI LGBT Rights Officer and produced by the Union of Students in Ireland in 2009. Can you identify any common trends or feelings evident in the testimonies?

Describe the role of the youth worker in supporting a young person who is coming out.

Homophobic bullying:
Homophobic bullying is bullying based on prejudice against LGBT people, towards people who are or are perceived to be LGBT or against friends and family of LGBT people. Homophobic bullying can be used in the context of more general bullying against any young person at all. It is similar to all forms of bullying and includes:

- Verbal abuse – name-calling, jokes and teasing. Includes the use of the word 'gay' in a negative way.
- Non-verbal abuse – such as gesture or mimicry; also includes ignoring, excluding and isolating the person.
- Threatening behaviour – both verbal and non-verbal.
- Physical assault – punching, beating, kicking and so on.
- Spreading rumours
- Anti-LGBT graffiti, images and notes
- Cyber-bullying – including texting, posting material on social networking sites and malicious phone calls.

The seriousness of homophobic bullying cannot be overstated as can be deduced from the figures revealed in the 2009 study referred to earlier.

Legislation:

- Equal Status
- Employment Equality
- Education Act

Because homosexuality was only decriminalised in 1993, and education services were largely overseen by the Catholic Church (which even now does not accept the practice of homosexuality) the choices of LGBT people have been and continue to be very restricted and their lives overshadowed. One of the many results of this is difficulty in establishing what proportion of the population is LGBT, estimated to be somewhere between 5 and 10%. Put simply, if you are working with a group of ten young people, chances are that at least one of them will be LGBT. While the law now reflects a more enlightened approach in many areas, and discrimination against people based on their sexual orientation is now outlawed, it takes time and education to change people's attitudes.

How youth workers can support LGBT young people:

It is in the remit of the youth worker to educate and support all young people regardless of their sexual orientation.

In doing this, the youth worker or youth service should:

- Recognise the diversity of the group by using posters, promotional material and leaflets. Make LGBT a visible issue in your service.
- Acknowledge the LGBT young people in the group.
- Affirm the value of diversity.
- Model a positive attitude and appropriate behaviour.
- Challenge prejudice and stereotyping.
- Support young people who come out or are coming out.
- Take action to combat homophobic bullying in all its forms.

Any organisation providing services for young people should have clear policies and procedures to cover all aspects of sexual orientation and related concerns.

All staff and volunteers (including managers) should not only be offered training, but should be expected to attend training.

This excerpt from a *Rolling Stone* article highlights the real dangers of homophobic bullying but also the need for clear policies and procedures.

> *After nine suicides, a federal lawsuit, and the glare of the media spotlight, Minnesota's Anoka-Hennepin school district has at last rid itself of the policy that helped create a virulently anti-gay environment in its schools. In a 5–1 vote on Monday night, the district's school board repealed its Sexual Orientation Curriculum Policy, which required teachers to be 'neutral' on homosexuality. Teachers throughout the district had been so confused about how to enforce the policy that they'd avoided any mention of homosexuality, even when it meant ignoring anti-gay bullying; the result was a toxic environment in which LGBT students were marginalized, demoralized, and subjected to unchecked torment.* (www.rollingstone.com/politics Feb 2012)

References, resources and further reading

NYCI and Youth Net, 2012, *Access All Areas: A Diversity Toolkit for the Youth Work Sector*, Dublin: NYCI and Youth Net. See Section 3, 'Working with LGBT Young People'. This Toolkit has guidelines for working with a variety of marginalised young people.

Maycock, P., Bryan, A., Carr, N. & Kitching, K., 2009, *Supporting LGBT Lives: A Study of the Mental Health and Well-Being of Lesbian, Gay, Bisexual and Transgender People*, Dublin: GLEN & BeLonG To.

The organisations listed below have resources, training packages and supports throughout the country or can supply links to fellow organisations that will provide supports:

www.belongto.org
www.glen.ie
www.lgbt.ie

Young People in Families and Family Law

Demography
Definition of family
Changing family forms
Young people as parents
Marriage
Nullity, separation and divorce
Children and divorce
Unmarried parents
Rights and duties of parents and guardians
Registration of births
Civil Partnership
Domestic violence
Implications of family circumstances for youth work

Demography

The consideration of any issue, service or approach to youth work and young people must first take account of the nature and extent of the population that is under consideration.

General statistics are available from the Office of Central Statistics at www.cso.ie

Demography: the study of patterns and characteristics of human populations. In this case the study of the young population of Ireland.

It is not just the number of young people in total that influences current issues and services but also the proportion of young people in the population and the density of young people in any one area. The following tables show that around 10% of the population between the ages of 16 and 18 live in the Dublin City area. Even when towns of similar size are compared, the proportion of young people can vary widely.

Table 1.2.1 Different populations 2006

Age	Dublin City	Monaghan	Connaught	Mayo
16	5238	881	6836	1820
17	5302	836	7122	1807
18	6274	842	7291	1773
Total	16814	2559	21249	5400

Table 1.2.2 Different towns

2006 15–24 years			
Bray	4952	V	Mallow	1401
Roscommon	683	V	Enniscorthy	1468

Table 1.2.3 Proportion of population

Age	2006
0–14	20.5%
15–24	15.1%
25–49	38.0%
50–64	15.4%
67–79	8.3%

(Only former Yugoslav republic has a higher proportion in the 15–24 range.)

For example, while Bray and Mallow have a similar total population size, Bray has almost four times the number of people between the ages of 15 and 24.

When compared to Europe, Ireland has a higher proportion of young people between 15 and 24; Europe has an average of 12.7% in the 27 EU countries compared to 15.1% in Ireland.

Activity:

- Go to www.cso.ie.
- In the top right-hand search box, type 'interactive tables'.
- When the options come up, click on 'Interactive tables-CSO-Interactive Tables'.
- Next click on 2006 Index (or 2011 Index when it becomes available).
- Two columns will appear: 'Folders' and 'Census'
- In the first column, click on the + sign beside the word 'demography', then + census, then +2006 Small Area Population Statistics, then +SAPS Themes by Alphabetical List of Towns, then click on Theme 1;
- In the second column, two options will appear. For now click on the first one, Theme 1.1; a list of towns will appear, scroll down to the one that interests you. If you then click on the word 'Total' in the second column, you will get a breakdown of every age group. For example, you can see that in 2006 there were 29 young people aged 17 in Abbeyfeale in Limerick: 17 males and 12 females.

	0–14 years	15–24 years	24–29 years	Total
Local area/town				
Local Authority area				

Find out the number of young people in your area and the wider local authority catchment area.

Definition of family

The definition of the family used by the UN and broadly reflected in many sociological studies is as follows:

'Any combination of two or more persons who are bound together by ties of mutual consent, birth and/or adoption or placement and who together assume responsibility for, *inter alia,* the care and maintenance of group members through procreation or adoption, the socialisation of children and the social control of members.'

The constitutional definition of families in Ireland includes only those based on marriage:

> Article 41.1.1
> 'The State recognises the Family as the natural primary and fundamental unit group of Society, and as a moral institution possessing inalienable and imprescriptible rights, antecedent and superior to all positive law'.

> Article 41.3.1
> 'The State pledges itself to guard with special care the institution of Marriage, on which the family is founded and to protect it against attacks.'

Whatever the definition or view of the family, it is the primary agent of socialisation for children. Socialisation is the process by which human beings learn the values, rules and expectations of the society in which they live. While it is recognised that secondary agents of socialisation – peer group, community, clubs, and the media, for example – are becoming increasingly important to the young person, the family continues to be a central influence, and the young person's ongoing experience of family life has a huge impact on peer relationships and how the young adult emerges.

Changing family forms

An examination of census figures may yield a better understanding of the forms and types of families in which young people in modern Ireland are living.

The tables overleaf give some idea of the extent of that diversity and suggests that the notion of 'normal' fixed family life experience no longer exists, if it ever did.

Private households with no children are not included in this table, although childless households are the fastest growing family type in Ireland. See cso.ie for Census figures.

An examination of the figures from the 2002, 2006 and 2011 Censuses reveals that there is considerable and increasing diversity in family structures and forms in modern Ireland. The traditional family form of husband, wife and child(ren) has decreased significantly in the last decade and accounts for only 31.5% in the most recent census; this is down from 35.9% in 2002. The percentage of cohabiting couples has increased (from 2.28% in 2002 to just under 3% in 2011) as has the percentage of lone parents with children (from 11.7% to 12% in the same period).

Same-sex parents with children were included in the 2011 census for the first time numbering 230, and this is believed to be an underestimate. See Table 1.2.4.

The increasing need to recognise the diversity in family forms is also evidenced by the fact that a number of national organisations, such as One Family, Treoir and Marriage Equality, focus on the need for constitutional change in order to afford equal rights to all families regardless of type or structure.

Table 1.2.4 Composition of private households

	2002	2006	2011
Husband and wife with children (any age)	462,283 (35.9%)	477,705 (32.5%)	522,959 (31.5%)
Lone mother with children (any age)	111,878 (8.7%)	130,853 (8.9)	155,264 (9.9%)
Husband, wife, children (any age) and others	41,819 (3.24%)	28,247 (1.9%)	26,226 (1.6%)
Cohabiting couple with children (any age)	27,188 (2.1%)	39,626 (2.7%)	54,911 (3.3%)
Lone father with children (any age)	19,313 (1.5%)	21,689 (1.8%)	24,497 (1.5%)
Lone mother with children (any age) and others	15,785 (1.22%)	13,994 (0.95%)	15,190 (0.9%)
Lone father with children (any age) and others	3,658 (0.28%)	3244 (0.22%)	2,986 (0.9%)
Cohabiting couple with children (any age) and others	2,445 (0.18%)	3,467 (0.24%)	4,233 (0.3%)
Same-sex parents with children	—	—	230
Total private households	1,287,958	1,469,521	1,654,208

One Family – the national membership organisation of one-parent families
Treoir – the national information centre for parents who are not married to each other

Marriage Equality – an organisation that lobbies for recognition of and equal rights for families with same-sex parents.

Table 1.2.5: Children living with a lone parent enumerated by child's age

	2002	**2006**	**2011**
0–4 years	33,958	50,652	45,129
5–9 years	37,528	52,410	54,981
10–14 years	42,890	48,950	58,657
15–19 years	47,162	50,340	55,867
20–24 years	35,812	35,918	40,075

There have been other significant changes to family life in Ireland in the last 50 years or so.

The increasing participation of women in the workforce can mean that children experience more care from people outside the immediate family, e.g. in a crèche or with a child-minder. There are pros and cons of women working outside the home, as it can also mean less poverty and more material comforts due to a second income in a two-parent household.

A falling birth rate means that children in families today have fewer siblings to relate to and to look after or be looked after by. It may also mean that individual children get more attention from parents.

A fluctuating marriage rate and increasing numbers of children being born outside of marriage is in part a result of couples getting married later in life, and many having children prior to marriage. The proportion of children born to parents who are not married has hovered around one-third for a number of years. See tables overleaf.

Because the family in whatever form remains the primary socialising unit for children, the changes that occur within families between the birth of the child and their reaching independent adulthood have a significant effect on the emotional and psychological well-being of the young person. The existence of a stable and secure environment is an essential element in a child's development. This includes the emotional environment and the relationships that the child experiences while growing up. A significant factor in this is family breakdown and/or reconstruction.

Table 1.2.6 Number of persons in private households by age

	2002	**2006**	**2011**
under 5 years	273,610	300,246	337,240
5–12 years	431,350	450,720	487,782
13–18 years	361,420	340,367	329,742

Table 1.2.7 Children living with one or both parents by age (CSO Volume 3 Table 33 G)

With both parents	**2002**	**2006**	**2011**
0–4 years	216,777	242,653	290,140
5–9 years	213,949	229,605	253,305
10–14 years	232,182	218,185	232,133
15–19 years	238,567	211,695	203,942
20–24 years	166,538	148,252	147,347

Firstly let us consider the lone-parent family. While an increasing number of children are being brought up by lone parents, this may not be the case throughout a child's life. Consider the following scenario:

Scenario:

Sarah had her first baby, John, when she was 17 and living with her parents. John's father, Mark, remained involved for a short time, but then the couple lost contact when he moved to another part of the country. When Sarah was 19, she had another baby, Kevin. The relationship between Sarah and Kevin's father ended before he was born.

Sarah's family home was now quite overcrowded, and Sarah was housed nearby with her two children.

After a time, Sarah met Nick, and when John was five years old, the couple moved in together. They subsequently had two daughters over the next five years, but then Nick lost his job, the relationship deteriorated and finally ended when John was twelve and the youngest baby two years old. At present, Sarah has developed a new relationship with Ian; Ian is committed to Sarah and the children but neither wants to rush into things, particularly because John is very antagonistic towards Ian and the relationship. Just recently, John has been badgering Sarah about making contact with his father, Mark. To complicate matters, Ian has two children from a previous relationship with whom he keeps in close contact.

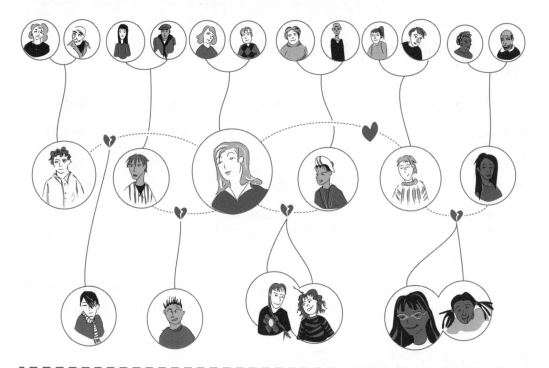

 Activity:

Draw a timeline of John's life marking out changes in his experience of family life in the previous scenario.

How children experience changes and how they cope with their experiences depends on a number of factors, not least how supportive their parents manage to be. Many parents find it difficult to support their children through emotional upheavals when they themselves are going through a traumatic period. Relationship breakdowns often mean practical changes for the children including moving house, changing school and friends and being less well-off financially. Contact with the absent parent is often fraught with tensions and disappointments. Although research shows that all the factors mentioned influence how a child copes, adolescents find changes in family structure more difficult than younger children, and boys find it most difficult of all. Family breakdown has always been a feature of family life in Ireland, but since divorce was introduced in 1997 there has been legal recognition of those breakdowns that also facilitates the establishment of stepfamilies and second families. In the UK, stepfamilies have been described as the fastest-growing family form. Principal statistics show births, marriages, deaths, divorce figures, and give some indication of the level of marriage breakdown, but there are to date no studies that reveal how many children are living in 'blended families' in Ireland.

> Blended families are family units in which one or both of the couple have children with other partners, and may have children together, all of whom share in the life of the family.

The longitudinal study 'Growing Up in Ireland' is looking at the lives of 8,500 children, and began when they were 9 years old in 2007/2008. The follow-up report was published in 2012 when the children were 13 years old, and the same will be done every four years. This will be an invaluable source of information on many aspects of the lives of young people in Ireland including their experience of family life and the changes therein.

 Activity:

Go to the 'Growing Up in Ireland' website and examine the family structures and family forms of the children, note the percentage of children who have experienced changes in their families since the study began.

Young people as parents

Another very important group that is growing in numbers each year is young persons who themselves are parents. In the 2006 census there was a total of 4,662 people under age 20 who were counted as parents; 1,956 (42%) of these were enumerated as lone parents, and a further 46.3% were cohabiting.

Table 1.2.8 Persons enumerated as lone parents

		2002	2006	2011
15–19 years	male	8	76	39
	female	642	1,889	1,491
20–24 years	male	147	323	251
	female	7,014	13,483	12,003

Table 1.2.9 Persons enumerated as couples

		2002	2006	2011
15–19 years	married male	107	159	323
	married female	328	379	520
	cohabiting male	353	550	NA*
	cohabiting female	1,112	1,609	NA
20–24 years	married male	1,939	2,616	2,930
	married female	5,136	6,372	6,452
	cohabiting male	8,070	21,282	NA
	cohabiting female	14,602	36,681	NA

NA: not available at time of going to print.

Research suggests that particularly in the case of younger couples, cohabitation seems to be more transitory than marriage, so these figures would indicate that a sizeable proportion of children born in Ireland to young parents will experience changes in family structure at some point. The tables above show that the number of lone parents is growing significantly, and within that, the number of lone fathers, although still small by comparison with lone mothers, is also increasing.

The experience of a young parent is influenced by many factors, including their living situation, their financial situation and their relationship with the other parent. Early research in Ireland suggested that young mothers tend to be afforded more 'adult' status than they were before they had children. The situation of young fathers appears to be very different, and in fact little research has been done in this area. One study done on young disadvantaged fathers (Corcoran, 2005) paints a bleak picture of young men who, if they are interested in the child at all, are alienated and often 'allowed' only occasional access and asked for some financial support. Figures from the Department of Social Protection suggest that about 20% of children born to young unmarried parents do not have the father's name on the birth certificate. Anecdotally, this seems to be because mothers are afraid that to do so would give the fathers more rights to interfere later on, or will render the mother ineligible for lone parent's allowance, even though this is not the case. Certainly, not placing a father's name on the birth certificate is a two-edged sword; on the one hand it facilitates the exclusion of the father, and on the other, it allows fathers to shrug off any responsibility they might feel more easily.

Crucially, from the child's point of view, not having their father's name on their birth certificate denies them one of their fundamental rights. Under Article 7 of the UN Convention on the Rights of the Child, children are granted 'as far as possible the right to know and be cared for by his or her parents'. At the time of writing, this was in the process of changing.

Marriage

Under the Irish Family Law Act 1995, in order for a marriage to be valid, both parties must be 18 years old, and three months' written notice of the intention to marry must have been given to the Registrar where the marriage is due to take place. Most religious denominations have premises registered for the administration of civil marriages but there may be additional denominational regulations which have no bearing on the civil legality of the marriage. In addition to the legal requirements outlined above, other conditions must be fulfilled in order for a marriage to be deemed valid. These are as follows:

- Each party must be free to marry.
- Each must be of sound mind and aware of what the marriage contract means.
- Neither party must be forced to marry against his or her will.
- One person must be female and one male.
- The parties must not be more closely related than first cousins.
- Regulations regarding residency and recognition of foreign divorces must be adhered to.

If a marriage does not work out there are now three options available in Ireland to a couple choosing to end their civil contract and to split up:

- Nullity
- Separation
- Divorce

Nullity, separation and divorce

Nullity

An annulment is a declaration that the marriage never actually existed. There are six grounds for establishing nullity and they are related to the regulations governing marriage. The six grounds are as follows:

1 There was an already existing valid marriage.
2 One or both were underage at the time of the marriage.
3 The formalities were not adhered to, e.g. three months' notice was not given.
4 Full consent was absent, e.g. they were forced or tricked into the marriage.
5 They were too closely related.
6 They were both the same sex, that is two men or two women.

Marriages may also be annulled if facts emerge at a later date which would have had an influence over either party's decision at the time of the marriage, for example if a past psychiatric history was concealed.

Separation

Separation may be by order of a court (a judicial separation) or by agreement between the couple without recourse to any law.

Either a mutual agreement or a judicial separation merely means that the husband and wife no longer have to live together. They are not free to marry another person and they are free to be reconciled.

The grounds for a **judicial separation** are:

- Adultery
- Unreasonable behaviour
- One year's continuous desertion
- One year's separation with consent, or three years without consent
- No normal sexual relationship for at least a year
- Indisposition

In some cases a combination of these grounds may exist.

Divorce

Divorce gives legal recognition to the fact that a marriage has irretrievably broken down and no longer exists in anything but name. It gives both parties the right to remarry if they so wish.

In Ireland, all four of the following conditions must be fulfilled in order to obtain a divorce:

1 The spouses have lived apart for at least four of the preceding five years.
2 There is no reasonable prospect of reconciliation.
3 Both spouses and any dependent children have been properly provided for.
4 Either spouse lived in Ireland when the proceedings began (or lived here for at least a year before that date).

Children and divorce

If a couple divorces the court will always make orders relating to the children. Matters such as **custody**, **access**, **guardianship** and **maintenance** of children will invariably have been dealt with in some manner by the couple, given that they must be living apart for at least four years before a divorce can be granted. See overleaf for details. The court may request reports to be made about any issues that affect the children's welfare.

Legal Aid is available to couples who cannot afford to pay legal fees.

Marital breakdown has serious consequences for children. It is generally recognised that it is not the separation or the divorce that causes problems for the children, it is rather the problems and friction that preceded it, combined with how the parents deal with the split afterwards. How children react to and cope with disruption to family life depends on how their needs have been met prior to and during the upheaval. It also depends on the nature of the marital split, i.e. whether it was reasonable and amicable or involved aggressive rows and animosity. Research indicates that all children are affected by the separation of their parents, and some children are severely damaged. Parental and family breakup combined with adolescence can be intensely traumatic. Children may experience some or all of the following prior to, during and/or after the breakdown, depending on their personality, the nature of the split and their age and stage of development:

- grief
- anger
- resentment
- denial
- sadness and loss
- insecurity

- relief
- emotional distress
- behavioural difficulties

The effects of the above may be long lasting, resulting in poor performance at school and work; children may also have difficulties in their future relationships as adults. There are also significant negative after-effects for the 'absent' parent (the parent who no longer lives with the children on a daily basis), who is more likely to lose contact with the family, and the family may be less well-off materially as a result of the breakdown.

When parents are helped to manage their problems, conflicts and separation in a positive way, it is more likely that the children will be better able to cope with the situation. Some recent studies suggest that it is less harmful for children to live with two parents who are not getting on than for those two parents to separate; however, other studies suggest just as strongly that it very much depends on the nature of the family relationships.

The government is committed to providing support for couples and their families who are separating and the following measures are in place:

- **The Family Support Agency** aims to promote and support families and to prevent family breakdown.
- **Legal Aid** has been increased, both in terms of expansion of the numbers of centres and in terms of who is eligible.
- **A Family Mediation Service** is a free service that is available to separating couples to help them sort out their affairs agreeably so that the trauma and disruption to the children can be kept to a minimum.

Unmarried parents

When a child's parents are not married to each other, the child has rights pertaining to both parents, including rights to maintenance and inheritance. These rights are laid out in the Guardianship of Infants Act 1964, which was the first piece of modern Irish legislation to address the needs of children born outside of marriage or in the event of marriage breakdown.

The Status of Children Act 1987
- abolished the concept of illegitimacy
- gave unmarried fathers legal rights to be appointed guardians or to seek access and/or custody
- provided for the establishment of paternity through presumption, declaration or blood test
- updated and extended the law in relation to maintenance payments.

The Children Act 1997 further amended and expanded the law with regard to guardianship, custody, access and maintenance.

Rights and duties of parents and guardians

Guardianship

A guardian is a person who has legal rights and duties in respect of a child. The guardian is entitled to have a say in all decisions relating to the child's upbringing, including:
- where and with whom the child lives
- choice of school
- consent to medical treatment
- consent for passport application
- religious upbringing
- consent to adoption
- responsibility to ensure the provision of adequate care.

A mother is always and automatically a guardian. Under the Children Act 1997, an unmarried father can become guardian of his child without going to court, provided that the mother and father sign a sworn agreement to this effect. Otherwise, the father must apply to the local district court to be appointed a guardian, which might involve proof of his paternity. When a marriage breaks down, both parents may retain joint guardianship, or the court may appoint just one parent as guardian or appoint an independent guardian.

Custody

The person or persons who have custody of a child have charge and care of the child on a day-to-day basis. The mother of a child born outside marriage has sole custody of the child and the father must apply to the courts for formal custody. The 1997 Act allows for joint custody orders to be made.

Access

When one parent has full custody of the child, the other parent can apply for access to visit the child regularly or at specified times. The 1997 Act allows that other persons, such as grandparents, may also apply to the courts for access.

Maintenance

Maintenance refers to the payments made by one person to another towards the children's cost of living. Unmarried parents do not have a responsibility to maintain each other. Maintenance can be voluntary or by order of the court. Orders made by the courts will take into consideration the earnings of the person against whom the order is being made. Paying maintenance **does not** give any rights of access or guardianship.

Except where parents are in agreement, all decisions about guardianship, custody and access are made by the court, with the first and primary consideration being given to the child's interests and welfare. While the mother's views will be considered in making a decision about any of the above, the court may grant an order in favour of the father without the mother's agreement.

When unmarried parents are having difficulty agreeing on shared parenting issues such as times of access or the amount of maintenance, the Family Mediation Service may be an alternative to going to court (which is expensive and tends to be confrontational).

There are many positives to be gained from going to mediation, including that:
- it encourages and supports co-operation between the parents;
- it allows parents to be in charge of their own decisions;
- it promotes partnership and positive communication.

Registration of births

By law, the birth of a child must be registered within three months of the birth and a surname must be chosen for the child.

- When a mother is married there is a presumption in law that her husband is the father of the child and the birth will be registered in both parents' names automatically.

- If the parents are not married to one another, both parents can go together to the Registrar's office to place the father's name in the Register of Births. (See note below re: proposal from the Law Reform Commission.) Alternatively, one parent can bring a statutory declaration with them that names the father of the child.

- If the child has been registered in the mother's name alone, it is possible to re-register at any date in order to place the father's name on the birth certificate. If the mother is married but the child's father is not her husband, her husband must sign a declaration that he is not the father before another man's name can be entered on the certificate.

  The entering of the father's name on the birth certificate does not confer guardianship, access or custodial rights. It is just proof of paternity as stated earlier.

- Where parents marry after the birth, the child automatically becomes a child of the marriage and there is no requirement to re-register if the father's name is already entered into the Register. Additionally, on marrying the mother, the father automatically becomes a joint guardian of his child.

- If the mother subsequently marries another man, any orders made in favour of the father will remain in force. If the new couple wants the husband to adopt the child, then the father's consent will be required if he has been appointed guardian/custodian.

  The Law Reform Commission proposes (2012) the following system for a non-marital father to register his name on the birth certificate of a child in the absence of agreement with the mother. The father can make an application to the relevant Registrar of Births to be entered on the birth certificate as the father of the child. The Registrar would record the application and inform the mother of the child that the application has been made. The mother would then have 28 days to object to the name of the man being entered on the birth certificate as the father of the child. If no objection were made, a final entry of the father's name would be entered on the birth certificate. If the mother were to make an objection, the Registrar of Births would refer the matter to the District Court, whose only power would be to delete the entry if it were established by the mother that the man was not the father of the child. The Commission also recommends that there be a similar process to enable the mother of a child to enter the name of a man on the birth certificate as the father of the child without agreement. The mother can inform the Registrar of the name of the alleged father of the child. The Registrar would then contact the man and he would have 28 days within which to raise an objection to his name being entered on the birth certificate. Again, the District Court would, on appeal, determine the issue if there was a dispute.

Establishing Paternity

If a man's name is on a child's birth certificate, then paternity is presumed. If there is a court order for maintenance, access, custody or guardianship which names the father, then that is accepted as proof. If there is a dispute, then a paternity test can be done. A court order can be obtained in respect of this if it is not undertaken voluntarily. A positive paternity test does not automatically confer any rights in respect of that paternity, i.e. the man will still have to apply through the courts for access, etc.

Civil Partnership

The Civil Partnership and Certain Rights and Obligations of Cohabitants Act 2010 brought about major changes to Irish law regarding families and relationships. It recognised for the first time the relationships of same-sex couples and unmarried, cohabiting couples whether they are same-sex or opposite-sex. Under the new laws introduced in 2010 any two unmarried adults of the same sex can enter into a Civil Partnership. Civil Partnership extends a number of rights and responsibilities to same-sex couples which had previously only been available to opposite-sex couples in marriage. It covers areas such as protection from domestic abuse, the recognition of foreign civil partnerships and same-sex marriages as civil partnerships, inheritance and the dissolution of a relationship. Perhaps the most important aspect of Civil Partnership is that the partners are formally recognised as 'next of kin' in the eyes of the law. For example, if one partner is seriously ill or hospitalised, the other partner is allowed to visit them and to have a say in what medical treatment they should receive if the patient is unable to decide for themselves. Though civil partnerships are commonly regarded as being 'just like marriage' there are a number of key differences. The 2011 report by Marriage Equality, 'Missing Pieces', found 169 legal differences between marriage and civil partnerships. The most disappointing failure of the Act, for many, was the lack of provision for children. Any children of a couple in a civil partnership do not, in legal terms, have two same-sex parents but rather one parent (either adoptive or biological) and no legal relationship to the second adult in the household. Should the legal parent die or desert the family, the children have no automatic right to their second parent. In the event of relationship breakdown, the second parent cannot apply for custody or guardianship, although they can hope for 'access'. As well as providing for same-sex couples who wished to formalise their relationship under the law, the Civil Partnership and Certain Rights and Obligations of Cohabitants Act 2010 contains a redress system for cohabiting couples who have lived together in an intimate relationship for at least five years, or two years if there is a child.

Domestic violence

Domestic violence refers to violence in the home perpetrated by adults against their partners, parents and/or children. The most common forms of abuse are emotional, physical and sexual, and all abuse occurs across all social classes. The extent of domestic violence is difficult to gauge as it is grossly under-reported. Women are slow to report incidents often for fear of reprisals but also because they often feel that they have no hope of escaping the relationship. Men may be slow to report for the same reasons, but also because of fear of ridicule. Domestic violence may also be under-reported because people find it difficult to admit that their relationship is abusive.

Any attempt to reduce domestic violence must address gender issues and power imbalances in society, all of which is an area of concern in youth work practice.

Cosc (the National Office for the Prevention of Domestic, Sexual and Gender-based Violence) was established in June 2007 with the key responsibility of ensuring the delivery of a well coordinated 'whole of Government' response to domestic, sexual and gender-based violence against women and men. One of Cosc's primary tasks has been the development of a National Strategy on Domestic, Sexual and Gender-based Violence. The strategy was approved by the government in 2010 and Cosc will now focus on ensuring its implementation.

The Domestic Violence Act 1996 has gone some way towards increasing protection for adults and children who experience abuse. The main provisions of the Act are as follows:

- The law has been extended to cover any adult with whom the person shares residence, not just a spouse.
- Power has been given to the Department of Health and Children to apply for protection on behalf of a person.

- If a person breaks the law, for example by ignoring a Barring Order, they can now be arrested without need for a warrant.

Under the 1996 Act, four types of court order can be obtained to protect a spouse, partner, dependent child or persons in other domestic relationships:

- A Safety Order prevents the person named from using or threatening to use violence against the applicant, molesting or frightening the applicant. If the applicant lives in the same house, the respondent (the allegedly abusive person) does not have to leave. It is effective for five years.
- A Protection Order has the same effect as a Safety Order, but it is an interim order that is effective until a decision on another order can be made.
- An Interim Barring Order and Barring Order both require the respondent to leave the shared home.
- The Domestic Violence (Amendment) Act 2002 directs that the respondent be notified of the order and the reasons as soon as possible. When made *ex parte* (without the respondent being present in the court) the order must be confirmed or rescinded within eight days.

Application by Health Authorities

The Domestic Violence Act empowers the Health Authorities to apply for an order to protect a person of any age if they believe that person to be in danger and unable to pursue an application for a Barring or Safety Order themselves, perhaps because of fear.

Implications of family circumstances for youth work

The beginning of this section covered demographics because an understanding of same is obviously necessary in planning, but also because in evaluating services, youth workers must be aware of the nature and size of the population in their local area.

Every young person has a family background and it is essential to see young people in the context of their family as it gives insight into the supports and stresses that they have in their lives.

The basics of family law are laid out here, and there are signposts to the resources that are available. Youth workers should access accurate information on aspects of family law both in order to be aware of any implications for young people in their service regarding access, guardianship, barring orders, etc., and to be able to offer accurate guidance and appropriate support.

References, resources and further reading:

Corcoran, M., 2005, *Portrait of the 'Absent Father': The Impact of Non Residency on Developing and Maintaining a Fathering Role* in The Irish Journal of Sociology, Vol 14 (2), 2005, pp. 134–154

Donohoe, J. and F. Gaynor, 2011, *Education and Care in the Early Years* (4th ed.), Dublin: Gill and Macmillan.

Nestor, J., 2011, *An Introduction to Irish Family Law* (2nd ed.), Dublin: Gill and Macmillan.

Minister for Health and Children, 2006, *State of the Nation's Children*, Dublin: Department of Health and Children.

Growing Up In Ireland: National Longitudinal Study at www.growingup.ie

For general population statistics www.cso.ie

Treoir: Information for Unmarried Parents at www.treoir.ie

One Family Ireland: www.onefamily.ie

Bunreacht na hÉireann, 1937, Government Publications: Stationery Office

Education

Laws, issues and services

The Education Act 1998 is the main legislation that currently drives the education system in Ireland. Funding for education in Ireland is one of the lowest in the OECD (Organisation for Economic Cooperation and Development) countries. Education is compulsory for all children between the ages of 6 and 16. Parents can choose to educate their children outside the school system by home-schooling, but there is limited practical, official support for parents who choose this option. In practice, more parents choose home-schooling at the primary level, but will send their children to formal schooling for second level education because of the examination system.

Formal education is provided by the Department of Education and Skills (DES) at primary, secondary and third level. Education is provided, free of cost, at primary and secondary level. Although 'free', there are considerable costs attached to education – books, uniforms, so called 'voluntary' contributions and other extras, which can amount to considerable expense, particularly for large families. At primary and secondary level, supplementary welfare grants are available for those who are in receipt of long-term benefits or who can prove that the costs would cause undue hardship. At third level, a grant is available to individual students, but this is means tested.

The senior cycle at secondary level is not compulsory, as the child will have reached 16 years or completed the Junior Certificate cycle. The senior cycle lasts two or three years depending on whether the school offers a transition year programme. Almost three quarters of schools offer the transition year, but in many of these, individual students may opt to complete the cycle in two years by skipping transition year. During these final two years students have three options:

- **The Leaving Certificate** is the main basis on which entry requirements to third-level education is accessed.
- **The Leaving Certificate Vocational Programme** (LCVP), which focuses on technical and vocational areas.
- **Leaving Cert Applied** (LCA), which focuses on preparation for working and adult life.

 Activity:

Grants, allowances and costs change from year to year. In order to familiarise yourself with the costs of going to school, imagine you have a 15-year-old attending your local school in Junior Cert year and an 18-year-old starting college. Find out the costs of attending the secondary school. Brainstorm all of the costs, and contact the school for more information. What allowances, grants, etc., are available? For the older child, find out what college 'fees' apply, and whether your child may be entitled to a grant.

Educational disadvantage

Educational disadvantage must be combatted at many levels, quite apart from financial support to individual families who are experiencing hardship. Recent figures and research (ESRI, 2010) show that

- approximately 1,000 pupils per year fail to make the transition between primary and secondary school despite the law on school-leaving age.
- about 11% of students have significant literacy problems on leaving school.
- pupils who live in disadvantaged areas experience severe literacy problems that are three times that of the national average.
- about 9,000 students or 20% leave school before the Leaving Certificate examination each year; about 3% leave school without any qualification at all.
- absenteeism is a common forerunner of dropping out.
- the nationwide average absentee rate is 14 days per year; in disadvantaged areas this increases to 21 days.

- children from areas of disadvantage are more likely to drop out.
- boys are more likely to drop out than girls. (ESRI, 2010)

There are many implications of dropping out, and students who do are more likely to:
- be unemployed;
- earn less;
- have lower standards of literacy and numeracy;
- become involved in crime, drug abuse and/or unplanned early parenthood.

Education and inequality

Young people from disadvantaged backgrounds don't do as well as those from more privileged backgrounds.

The secondary education system does not cater well for young people who have additional needs.

Some schools seem to take more than their fair share of pupils who have multiple additional needs.

The need to address the following issues of inequality has long been recognised:
- improving access to early education
- improving literacy and numeracy standards
- improving the involvement of parents and communities
- supporting school attendance and progression
- recognising the need for specifically trained, quality teachers for schools in areas of disadvantage
- monitoring and evaluation
- streaming, which definitely has a negative impact

The Education Act 1998 defines educational disadvantage as 'the impediments to education arising from social or economic disadvantage which prevents students from deriving appropriate benefit from education in Schools...' (Section 32(9) Early school-leaving or dropping out is related to the issue of educational disadvantage.

Activity:

Aim: to gain an insight into reasons for school drop out.
Profile an early school-leaver versus a student who successfully completes school.
Brainstorm all the characteristics of the two students and all the possible reasons behind their choices.
Following this, consider therefore what might be the optimum approach to encouraging students to return to or stay in school.

Combatting disadvantage and inequality

The Education and Welfare Act 2000 addresses the issue of early school-leaving, and in the past decade a number of schemes have been put in place in an effort to combat disadvantage. Many of the schemes and programmes outlined below involve the provision of extra resources to support the disadvantaged children, including extra classes, extra teachers and smaller classes. These fall under a broader programme for Social Inclusion funded and supported by the Department of Education and Skills called 'Social Inclusion – Delivering Equality of Opportunity in Schools'. More information on the schemes outlined here can be obtained on the Department's website www.education.ie.

- Home School Community Liaison Scheme aims to support students at risk of failing or dropping out through home visits by Liaison Officers who encourage the parents to support the child's education.
- School Completion Programme targets individual young people of school-going age, both in and out of school, and aims to address inequalities in education access, participation and outcomes.
- Support Teachers Project targets children whose learning is affected by their behaviour, which may be disruptive, disturbed or withdrawn. Support Teachers focus on social, emotional and personal development in working with children, and allow children to experience success in their school life by working on their strengths. Such work may require the curriculum to be adapted to suit the child's level of need.
- Giving Children an Even Break involves the provision of additional teaching and financial allocations to participating schools in order to combat

disadvantage; it means a reduction of class sizes in the participating schools and additional resources.

■ Breaking the Cycle seeks to discriminate in favour of schools in selected urban and rural areas which have high concentrations of children at risk of not reaching their potential in the education system because of their socio-economic backgrounds. Strategies include extra staff and additional funding and coordination.

■ Disadvantaged Area Scheme (DEIS) As part of this scheme, schools seeking disadvantaged status are assessed and prioritised as to need on the basis of socio-economic and educational indicators such as unemployment levels, housing, medical card status and information on basic literacy and numeracy. In addition, disadvantage assessments take account of pupil–teacher ratios. Support involves increase capitation grant and extra finance for materials and classroom equipment.

■ Literacy and Numeracy Schemes involve facilitating extra training of teachers to deliver programmes aimed at improving literacy and promoting mathematical skills. Programmes under this scheme include First Step, Reading Recovery and Maths Recovery.

Programmes for early school-leavers

Programmes such as the Vocational Training Opportunities Scheme, Youthreach and Post Leaving Certificate courses aim to improve young people's access to second-chance or alternative education.

■ VTOS is the Vocational Training Opportunities Scheme, which offers unemployed people an opportunity to return to structured learning in an adult setting. Applications for inclusion in the scheme is open to people who are over 21 years of age and who have been in receipt of a social welfare payment for over 6 months.

■ Youthreach is delivered through Centres for Education managed by Vocational Education Committees (www.ivea.ie). The programme is also delivered in a network of Community Training Centres funded by the Department of Social Protection and 'Justice Workshops' funded by the Department of Justice Equality and Law Reform. A parallel programme in a culturally appropriate setting is delivered in Senior Traveller Training Centres (www.sttc.ie).

The programme is directed at unemployed early school-leavers aged 15 to 20, and offers them the opportunity to identify and pursue viable options within adult life, and provides them with opportunities to acquire certification. It operates on a full-time, year-round basis.

■ Back to Education Initiative (BTEI): The Back to Education Initiative provides part-time Further Education programmes for young people and adults while allowing them to combine a return to learning with family, work and other responsibilities. Those in receipt of unemployment payments or means-tested social welfare benefits, and holders of medical cards and their dependants are entitled to free tuition.

The Back to Education Allowance is paid by Department of Social Protection to facilitate people to retain payments while participating in full-time education courses. For those on Jobseekers Allowance you must be over 21 years to qualify for BTEI, but some who have been on long-term allowances since age 16 may qualify at 18.

Education for children with additional needs

Education for children with additional needs may be provided in ordinary classes in mainstream schools, in special classes in mainstream schools or in special schools. In mainstream schools they may get help from learning support and resource teachers and from special needs assistants (SNAs). These supports for children with special educational needs are available in primary and post-primary schools.

Under the Education for Persons with Special Educational Needs Act 2004 each child assessed with a special educational need should have a personal education plan, though this has not yet been fully implemented. **The National Council for Special Education, Special Educational Needs Organisers (SENOs), the Special Education Support Service (SESS) and The National Educational Psychological Service (NEPS)** are the principle organisations and structures that support and co-ordinate services for children with additional needs.

There are also some extra resources for education of children from the Traveller community and for children for whom English is not their first language.

The recent recession has resulted in serious cutbacks in education generally but particularly to some of these programmes.

Education beyond secondary school

When their secondary education has ended, young Irish people have options to progress to further education courses, diploma, certificate and degree courses in Institutes of Technology and in universities. Post Leaving Certificate (PLC) courses are post-secondary education programmes of integrated general education, vocational training and work experience for young people and adults who have completed upper second-level education or equivalent. It is a one- or two-year full-time course designed to enhance students' employment prospects or progression to third-level education. Part-time options at this level are also available under the Back to Education Initiative (BTEI).

These courses offer students the opportunity to gain a FETAC Level 5 and 6 certificates in a broad range of vocational areas including youth work, art, dance, fashion design, childcare, hair and beauty and media studies. In the last few years it has been the fastest-growing education sector in Ireland and offers opportunities to those who

- wish to get back to education having left school early.
- want to acquire a vocational skill to enhance their employment opportunities.
- did not score enough points for a particular university course and want to try again through the FETAC entry route rather than repeating the Leaving Certificate.

Higher or third-level education: Higher education in Ireland consists of seven universities (with associated colleges of education), 14 Institutes of Technology and a number of private independent colleges. The universities and Institutes of Technology are autonomous and self-governing, but are substantially state-funded. The minimum academic entry requirements for the majority of third-level courses are determined at individual institution level and are generally based on national examination performance, namely CAO points and the Leaving Certificate.

The role of the youth worker in education

It is very important that youth workers be aware of the different schemes and educational avenues open to young people in their area. Young people may need individual advice and guidance and the service should be able to support them or point them in the right direction. Additionally, the youth service can be proactive by providing talks by career guidance services or other young adults who have been through the system. Careers, further education and training make excellent topics for peer education and provide focus for trips to colleges' open days. It is equally important that youth workers be good role models by embracing learning themselves, and by being positive and encouraging in all whenever the topics of school, learning and education come up.

Youth workers may also be in a position to notice that a young person is struggling, and may be able to arrange support and intervention at an early stage.

References, resources and further reading

More information can be obtained on the following websites:
Department of Education and Skills *www.education.ie*
The Irish Vocational Education Association *www.ivea.ie*
The National Coordinating Unit for Senior Travelling Training Centres *www.sttc.ie*
For information about careers and qualifications: *www.qualifax.ie*
www.springboardcourses.ie

For information about third-level courses and entry requirements:
www.cao.ie
Byrne, D. and E. Smyth, 2010, *No Way Back? The Dynamics of Early School Leaving*, Dublin: ESRI, NCCA and DES.

Employment

Employment regulations relevant to young people
Income, maintenance and welfare entitlements
Training and work experience schemes

Quite a number of young people engage in part-time work while still at secondary school and an even larger percentage undertake part-time work to finance themselves in further education. A significant number leave school at 16 and go straight into employment, and a further cohort dependent on income from parents or from the state are unemployed. In these recent times of economic hardship, an increasingly high proportion of young people under 25 all over Europe are in a state of extended unemployment.

Each year the budget introduces changes to allowances; economic pressure in the next few years may bring about other unforeseen changes. The main aim here, therefore, is to give a broad view as to how things stand at the time of writing. To facilitate updates of this information, a list of sources with associated activities is given so that youth workers can access up-to-date information for the young people with whom they are working.

Employment regulations relevant to young people

This is probably the area that is least likely to change, as these regulations were drawn up with the welfare and rights of young people in mind rather than in relation to any temporary economic issues or pressures. The relevant law is **The Protection of Young Persons (Employment) Act 1996.**

Anyone who is working has general rights in relation to their employment. The following are relevant to all young people, who if employed should receive:

- **a written contract of employment** within one month of taking up employment;
- **correct rates of pay and a payslip** – there are different rates of pay in relation to age groups particularly at the younger ages. The minimum wage applies to

all those 18 years or over; those under 18 must be paid at least 70% of the minimum wage rate;

- representation from a **Trades Union representation** if there are difficulties – in most workplaces the relevant Trade Union would have a shop steward or representative;
- **protection from bullying and sexual harassment** – regulations in relation to this should be posted in a public place;
- a summary of the **Protection of Young Persons (Employment) Act 1996;**
- a summary of the **Code of Practice** (in relation to young people employed in licensed premises).

Regulations regarding working hours

Children under 16 years:
- Must not work before 8.00 a.m. or after 8.00 p.m.
- During school term 14-year-olds must not work at all.
- For young people between the ages of 14 and 15 years, holiday work should consist of light work to a maximum of 7 hours in any 24-hour period and to a maximum of 35 hours in any one week.
- 15- to 16-year-olds should only work 8 hours per week during school term.

Children over 16 years:
- 16- to 17-year-olds must not work before 6.00 a.m. or after 10.00 a.m. except when employed in licensed premises, where they can work until 11.00 p.m.
- Must have at least 21 days off during school holidays.
- Must have two consecutive days off each week and 14 hours off in each 24-hour period.
- Workers are entitled to a rest break after four hours' work.

Employers:

Under the law employers have statutory duties in relation to young people in their employment. It is the employer's duty to examine the worker's birth certificate so that they are clear about the age of the young person, and if under 16 years, the young person must provide written permission from their parents indicating parental approval. Employers must keep records of all young people in their employ and of the starting and finishing times of those young people.

Complaints in relation to infringements of the Protection of Young Persons (Employment) Act 1996 may be referred to **The Inspection Services of the National Employment Rights Authority, Government Buildings, O'Brien Road, Carlow.**

Income, maintenance and welfare entitlements

Parents are responsible for the maintenance of a young person until they reach their eighteenth birthday. As a result, anyone who has left school at 16 years and is unemployed is not entitled to any payment from social welfare.

For a person aged 18–24 years, an application for social welfare payments is means-tested and assessed under 'benefit and privilege'.

> **Means test:** an assessment of all the sources of income a person has in order to assess whether they are eligible to receive income support. The means test may vary according to the kind of maintenance being applied for.

> **'Benefit and privilege'** is the assessment of the monetary value which living with parents has for a young person. It means that the parents' income is considered in the means test, which is then applied to all young persons under 25 years who are living with their parents. However it does not apply if the young person is married or if they have a dependent child.

Basically, the amount assessed as benefit and privilege is based the parents' income. It is likely that the amount and assessment will change from budget to budget, but can always be checked **www.citizensinformation.ie** or on the website of the **Department of Social Protection.**

If the young person has been living independently for three years and returns to their parents' home, the total 'Benefit and Privilege' is taken as €7.00 for assessment purposes at the time of writing.

If the young person has been working for two years and made PRSI contributions they may be entitled to **Jobseekers Benefit**, which is not means-tested or assessed under benefit and privilege.

There are numerous other payments that may be afforded to a young person who has health problems or additional needs. For example, a young person with a disability may get a **Disability Allowance** after their sixteenth birthday, but this is means-tested and their disability is assessed.

A **Supplementary Allowance** may be provided for a young person who is not supported by parents and is in need of urgent or emergency funds. The application is made to the local social welfare officer who usually operates out of the local health centre.

Regulations in relation to a young person who is living in Ireland but comes from another country

If that country is outside the EU and the young person is a(n):

- **Refugee**, they are entitled to the same assistance and assessment as an Irish person if they have been granted refugee status.
- **Asylum seeker** aged over 18 and accommodated in direct provision centres, they receive €19.60 per week. They are not allowed to seek employment.
- **Unaccompanied minor**, they must be under 18 years and have arrived in Ireland alone. They are placed in the care of the HSE, generally in direct provision centres. In this way, they are treated differently from Irish children who are out of home and in care.

If the young person is from another EU country: they are entitled to the same services as Irish young people, but must first prove that they have been living here or in the Common Travel Area for a certain length of time.

> The **Common Travel Area** refers to the UK, Channel Islands and Isle of Man and Ireland, a zone through which you can live and travel without a passport.

Training and work experience schemes:

There are usually a number of training and work experience schemes available for all unemployed people and some are especially aimed at the young and unemployed. At the moment these include:

- JobBridge – an internship/work experience scheme.
- Community Training Centres (CTC) offer training to early school-leavers.
- Local Training Initiatives (LTI) target young people who are 18–25 years old.

Details of payments, regulations and schemes change regularly and particularly after the Budget, which is published annually early in December. It is important to check that any information given out to young people is up to date.

References, resources and further reading

www.welfare.ie The Department of Social Protection website includes all the information in relation to all benefits and allowances. It also outlines rules of eligibility and payment rates. From 2012, the Department of Social Protection will be delivering a new integrated service for jobseekers following the merger with the Employment Services and Employment Programmes (formerly administered by FAS; see CTCs and LTIs above) and the Community Welfare Service (formerly with the HSE).

www.citizensinformation.ie This website is managed by the Citizens Information Board and includes information about rights and entitlements on all life events which people in Ireland experience. The information is available in several languages. The Citizens Information Board also publishes a resource pack with activities and quizzes that could be used by youth workers to educate young people about their rights on a number of issues.

www.youthworkireland.ie Youth Work Ireland runs a range of Youth Information Services throughout the country providing information on all aspects of life including rights and entitlements.

www.employmentrights.ie Covers a broad range of information on rights and entitlements for employees and employers.

www.revenue.ie Covers everything to do with tax, including forms and how to apply for a PPS number and tax rebates.

www.equality.ie Covers information on all issues relating to equality and steps to take if a person feels that they are being discriminated against.

www.entemp.ie Department of Enterprise, Trade and Innovation website covers a broad range of information on employment and enterprise.

www.spunout.ie Spunout is a youth-led media initiative covering all aspects of youth information such as health, lifestyle, travel, family and employment. The site lists all the services on a county-by-county basis.

Youth and Justice

Legislation

The Children Act 2001 is the main legislation governing children in the juvenile justice system in Ireland. The Act was amended by the Criminal Justice Act 2006 and The Child Care (Amendment) Act 2007

The Office of the Minister for Children and Youth Affairs has overall responsibility for development of policy in the area; there are three other departments involved, namely:

- The Department of Justice, Equality and Law Reform
- The Department of Education and Skills
- The Department of Health and Children

Under the legislation, the age of criminal responsibility has been raised to 12 years. Although it has been raised from 7 years, it remains one of the lowest in Europe. An exception is made for 10- and 11-year-olds charged with very serious offences, such as murder, rape or aggravated sexual assault. The Director of Public Prosecutions (DPP) must give consent for any child under the age of 14 years to be charged.

Legislation focuses on prevention, diversion and rehabilitation. The use of detention for a child is to be a last resort.

Activity:

In the group,

- list the crimes, misdemeanours and/or undesirable behaviours that you think are most commonly committed by young people.
- identify the victims.
- divide the list into behaviours that you consider to be criminal and not criminal.
- split the crimes into categories (e.g. vandalism, drug and alcohol use, anti-social behaviour, gangs, teen violence against teens, shoplifting, etc.) For each category, consider what factors might have lead the young people into these behaviours.
- consider who might be involved in terms of social class, gender, ethnic group.
- consider the risk factors for the young people involved, such as their family, school, community and/or peers. Who do the risk factors affect and how?

The Principles of the Children Act 2001

- Any child who accepts responsibility for his/her offending behaviour should be diverted from criminal proceedings, where appropriate.
- Children have rights and freedoms before the law equal to those enjoyed by adults and a right to be heard and to participate in any proceedings affecting them.
- It is desirable to allow the education of children to proceed without interruption.
- It is desirable to preserve and strengthen the relationship between children and their parents/family members.
- It is desirable to foster the ability of families to develop their own means of dealing with offending by their children.
- It is desirable to allow children to reside in their own homes.
- Any penalty imposed on a child should cause as little interference as possible to the child's legitimate activities, should promote the development of the child and should take the least restrictive form, as appropriate.

- Detention should be imposed as a last resort and may only be imposed if it is the only suitable way of dealing with the child.
- There should be due regard for the interests of the victim.
- A child's age and level of maturity may be taken into consideration as mitigating factors in determining a penalty.
- A child's privacy should be protected in any proceedings against him/her. (OMCYA, 2011)

The Irish Youth Justice Service

Set up in 2005, the Irish Youth Justice Service is the office responsible for services, policy and development. The following were introduced under the 2001 Act:
- The establishment of a Garda Diversion Programme.
- The establishment of a Children's Court.
- The introduction of a fines system.
- The introduction of a curfew.
- The introduction of court orders to compel parents to exercise proper control over their children.
- A limited 'clean-slate' approach in respect of most offences committed by children.
- Placing the burden of proof on parents whose children are found begging.
- Provisions in relation to safety of children at entertainments.
- Updating the law on abuse and exploitation.
- Establishment of a Special Residential Board (on a statutory basis).
- Introduction of family welfare conferences.
- The establishment of Children's Detention Services.

Garda Diversion Programme

There are two arms to this programme:
1 *The Garda Juvenile Diversion Programme* which operated informally since 1963 was formally established under the 2001 Act. The programme is implemented by Juvenile Liaison Officers (JLOs) while overall responsibility lies with the National Juvenile Office. The aim of the programme is to give children, particularly those between the ages of 12 and 17 years, a second chance by cautioning them, instead of entering them into the full justice

system. In short, when a child commits a crime, the relevant JLO will be alerted in order to assess whether the child is suitable for the programme; in order to be included the child must accept responsibility for his actions and agree to be cautioned and supervised. Following this, a Programme Conference will be convened where mediation and planning will take place. The child, his/her family and, if appropriate, the victim will all be involved in the conference.

2 *The Garda Youth Diversion Programmes* are local community-based projects which seek to divert young people away from activities and behaviours which are against the law. The projects offer opportunities for education, training, employment and the development of a range of talents and interests. The projects also aim to support healthy relationships between Gardaí and local communities.

In addition, there is also a **Schools Programme** involving visits by Gardaí to schools, both primary and secondary, to educate young people about crime, crime prevention and their rights and duties as citizens.

Another initiative is a programme called '**Copping On**', developed by Youthreach together with a network of Juvenile Liaison officers with the aim to raise awareness among young people about the consequences of criminal behaviour for everybody concerned. There are training resources and support available to various groups and agencies working with young people.

The Children's Court

The Children's Court is a special court held to deal with children who are in trouble with the law. The hearings are held separately to hearings held to try adults; in Dublin there is a special courtroom to hear children's cases; in other parts of the country the hearings are on special days or at special times. A particular effort is made to help children and their parents to understand and participate in what is going on. These courts are mostly held *in camera*.

Definition of *In Camera*
This legal term means 'in private'; there is no public access as there would be in a courtroom, and there is a limit on press reporting during these hearings.

Young Persons' Probation

Young Persons' Probation (YPP) is a division of the Probation Service. It aims to:
- help young offenders avoid re-offending;
- provide social work services;
- convene Family Conferences with young offenders, their families and victims on behalf of the Courts;
- implement Community Sanctions. These are used instead of detention and allow the child to remain in his/her community and in school or training. Parents and probation officers are expected to support the child in completing the sanction.

There are ten Community Sanctions available to the Courts, namely:

■ Community Service Order – A child of 16 or 17 years of age agrees to complete unpaid work in the community for a set total number of hours.

■ Day Centre Order – A child is ordered to go to a centre at set times and, as part of the order, to take part in a programme of activities.

■ Probation Order – Places a child under the supervision of the Probation Service for a period during which time the child must meet certain conditions set by the Court.

■ Training or Activities Order – A child is ordered to take part in and complete a programme of training or similar activity. The programme should be designed to help the child learn positive social values.

■ Intensive Supervision Order – A child is placed under the supervision of a named probation officer and has to attend a programme of education, training or treatment.

■ Residential Supervision Order – A child is placed in a suitable residential facility. The facility is to be close to where they normally live, attend school or go to work.

■ Suitable Person (Care and Supervision) Order – With the agreement of the child's parents or guardian, the child is placed in the care of a suitable adult.

■ Mentor (Family Support) Order – A person is assigned to help, advise and support the child and his/her family in trying to prevent the child from committing further offences.

- Restriction of Movement Order – Requires a child to stay away from certain places and to be at a specific address between 7 p.m. and 6 a.m. each day.
- Dual Order – Combines a Restriction of Movement Order with either supervision by a probation officer or attendance at a day centre.

– adapted from the OMYCA website

Restorative justice programmes:

There are two initiatives provided for under the Children Act 2001; one is a conference delivered through the Probation service and one is included under the Garda Juvenile Diversion Programme (see above).

In restorative justice, emphasis is placed on enabling the child to address the consequences of their actions by engaging with the victim. This could be by listening to the victim, making good the damage done, and/or apologising.

Detention

The courts will only sentence a child when all other options have failed or are not feasible – in other words, it will do so only as a last resort. This is extended to all children under 18 years and is the responsibility of the Minister for Justice, Equality and Law Reform. It is now illegal to sentence a young person under 18 years to prison.

There are currently four places of detention for young people; the most controversial is St Patrick's Institution, because it is managed by the prison service and is located close to Mountjoy Adult Prison Service. St Patrick's is a closed centre for young men aged between 16 and 21 years. Currently the main detention services and schools are all located in Lusk, Co. Dublin, and there are plans to develop these facilities to ensure an integrated and unified service to children who are remanded or committed by the courts. When it is completed, 16- and 17-year-olds will no longer be accommodated in St Patrick's Institution. The main focuses of these detention services are care, education and rehabilitation.

Anti-social Behaviour Orders (ASBOs)

ASBOs were introduced in 2007 under the Criminal Justice Act 2006. An ASBO is a civil order produced by the courts in conjunction with the Gardaí, which demands that a child (or adult) stop behaving in an anti-social manner. Anti-social behaviour is defined as anything that causes or is likely to cause the following:

- harassment;
- significant or persistent alarm, distress, fear or intimidation; or,
- significant or persistent impairment of their use or enjoyment of their property.

Behaviour warnings and ASBOs can be issued against any child between the ages of 12 and 18 years. The introduction of ASBOs was controversial and their use continues to be controversial, mainly because they are seen to blur the lines between civil and criminal law; it criminalises what is normal youthful behaviour and ignores the right of the child to privacy as the child's identity must be revealed in order to oversee compliance.

The Children's Rights Alliance, Youth Work Ireland and the National Youth Council of Ireland joined together and set up asbowatch.ie to monitor the use of ASBOs. More about the orders and the concerns can be found on that website.

References, resources and further reading

Lalor, K., de Róiste, Á., and M. Devlin, 2007, *Young People in Contemporary Ireland*, Dublin: Gill and Macmillan.

Children's Rights Alliance, Youth Work Ireland and the National Youth Council of Ireland *www.asbowatch.ie*

Irish Youth Justice Service *www.iyjs.ie*

Department of Children and Youth Affairs *www.dcya.gov.ie*

Youth Culture, Subculture and Globalisation

Culture

Subculture

The increase in subcultures today

Globalisation

The challenges for youth work

Culture

Different societies have different cultures. We learn the cultures of our society through a process called socialization. Socialisation is the process whereby human beings learn the rules, expectations, values, norms, language, etc., of the society in which they live. Primary socialisation occurs in the context of the family, and secondary socialization occurs when the individual begins to have contact with and be influenced by the wider community. In the context of the adolescent, the most significant group in the wider community is the peer group.

There are five major components of culture:

- Language – the way in which members of a group communicate and share meanings; it includes the use of jargon and slang.
- Symbols – representations of ideas by a group; this includes clothing, logos, flags and traditional arts.
- Values – the enduring concepts and ideals of a group. Values are driven by beliefs and influence the behaviour, emotions, thoughts and actions of a group.
- Norms – agreed ways of behaving correctly, and include common manners, such as how members of the group greet each other, or what is appropriate dress for an occasion.
- Material objects – all the goods and products that people use in their everyday life such as tools, cooking utensils, machines, decorations and musical objects. Material objects often give clues to the status of a person.

Activity:

Using the five headings on p. 66, make a chart identifying aspects of the culture of your native country and another country or culture that is familiar to you. Examine the similarities and differences between the two cultures.

Exercise: Norms are important! Try this – when you next get into a crowded lift, face the back wall instead of the doors. What happens?

Subculture

A group of people who make similar adaptations to some or all of the five components above constitute a *subculture* that distinguishes them as somewhat 'different', yet still part of the larger culture to which they belong. According to Paul Hodgkinson (2011), members of a subcultural group have:

- Commitment – this commitment should have at least a degree of influence on one's daily life in that time is spent interacting with like-minded friends in the real or the virtual world; the symbols and material artefacts of the subcultural group are used – things that might include clothing, posters and music.
- Identity – a sense of belonging to the group is felt and one is able to recognize others who belong.

■ Distinction – a sense of standing apart from other groups, having some values and beliefs that are unique to the group.

■ Autonomy – being independent of and from other groups.

In essence, a subculture brings together like-minded individuals who feel that elements of the major culture has little relevance to them and together they develop a sense of identity.

Subcultures can help the process of adolescent change, and can help individuals to cope and adapt to that change. Being part of a subcultural group is often seen as a necessary part of the journey from childhood to adulthood in the Western world where, in modern times, that change can happen very quickly.

Youth subcultures often manifest themselves in general themes such as:

* rebelling and rejecting the expectations of the adult world regarding work and conformity; rejecting the status quo.

* expressing their rebellion through a shared interest or a common activity – listening to/playing a specific type of music, drug use, fighting, creativity in the arts, political activism, experimenting with different religions, soccer hooliganism, online gaming and so on.

* claiming territory, as is typical of street gangs or different subcultures co-existing within a space, such as 'Goths' hanging out in a different space to the street dancers.

* moving in a tight social group outside of family; from a developmental stance, the subcultural group can lend a sense of security and support while the young person is trying to move away from the narrow confines of family.

* showing a distinctive and sometimes symbolic use of style and fashion. Nearly every subculture has a distinctive style, even if it's a question of what 'not to wear'.

* seeing mainstream society as banal, irrelevant or headed in the wrong direction leading to counterculture movements such as: the hippie movement of the '60s; the punk movement of the '70 and '80s; hip-hop and gangsta rap in the 1990s and 2000s; the Make Poverty History movement of the 00s and more recently the Occupy Wall Street movement. Of course, not all of these are purely youth movements, but they do seek to harness the energy and idealism of youth.

Activity:

Identify the major features of some youth subcultures (e.g. Goth, punk, etc.), such as:

- music both listened to and played.
- political associations, if any.
- peer influences including recognised leaders and followers and behaviour associated with the group.
- use of technology including mobile phones, laptops, particular online social networks.
- clothes and hair styles.
- patterns of behaviour such as use of drugs and alcohol, sexual behaviour, aggression including self-harm.

The increase in youth subcultures today

There are various theories to explain why there appear to be more youth cultures today than ever before, the most common of which are:

- The size of the society and the size of the youth group; where there is a large population there may be a need to be able to identify with a smaller group.
- The rate of change; in a society with a slow pace of change (such as traditional, pre-industrial societies) young people carry on much as their parents did, fitting into a relatively stable social context, whereas in a fast-moving society,

young people realise they cannot rely on the previous generation's way of coping, so they search for new ways and new identities that are more relevant. Youth subcultures help the dominant culture to evolve.

- The position of youth in our society; childhood and adolescence have grown longer in Western societies over the past 100 years so that young people do not consider themselves to be children and are not yet considered to be adults, and so are 'floating' and looking around for anchors for their identity. In line with theories of adolescent development, they are filled with excitement, energy and opinions. Many have lots of spare time and a fair proportion have expendable income.

- The impact of globalisation; it is easier for individuals and groups to see and interact with others who are like-minded even though they are not living in the same neighbourhood.

- Subcultural movements can spread more easily with the advent of new information technologies which, among other things, facilitate the use of social media.

Globalisation

Stiglitz (2002, p. 9) defines globalization as:

'…the closer integration of the countries and peoples of the world which has been brought about by the enormous reduction of costs of transportation and communication, and the breaking down of artificial barriers to the flows of goods, services, capital, knowledge and … people.'

Information, ideas, money and people move around the world quicker than ever before, and new language has sprung up to describe the phenomenon. The concept of the *global village* (a term coined by Marshall McLuhan in 1968) is used to describe how the world seems to be smaller through the use of information technology, particularly the Internet. *Global youth culture* refers to the fact that young all over the world from Sydney to Sao Paolo and from Kanturk to Kampala are listening to some of the same pop songs and rock bands, adopting similar styles of dress and can eat similar foods. Just as 'Google it' has become an equivalent term for 'look it up', 'McWorld' (Barber, 1992) aptly describes the rise of such popular culture. American cultural imperialism (sometimes broadly referred to as Westernisation) has dominated this global culture. Significant features of this Westernisation are individualism and consumerism.

'You're not going anywhere looking like that, young lady!'

> Individualism meaning the culture of the 'I', in which individual needs, attainments and independence are considered more important than those of the community.

> Consumerism is the drive to buy and use ever-increasing amounts of products, from food to clothing to the latest technology.

It can be argued that global youth culture has become the culture of individualism and consumerism.

Consumerism is being exploited by the economic interests of a handful of global enterprises and big industries, and the choices being made available to young people today is ever-increasing.

Young people in the Western world have huge buying power; they represent a significant part of the market in Europe as around 25% of the population in Europe is between the ages of 15 and 29 years (Eurostat, 2009). It is important to big business around the world that young people are helped to feel that they must have the latest gadget or fashion item to stay 'cool'. There is now a growing research field in business that involves 'Merchants of Cool' or 'Ambassadors of Cool' who seek to influence or discover the next 'cool' idea and be first to exploit that market. Businesses are aware that as soon as a product goes mainstream, it will soon cease to be 'cool' and so the cycle continues.

This business model affects youth populations in countries far removed from Western-style capitalism, with the culture of young people in a Peruvian or an Indian village being influenced by cultural artefacts that have little relevance to their lives.

The challenges for youth work

There are many issues associated with globalization but among the most challenging for youth work and youth workers in Ireland are:

1 How to develop a sense of identity and belonging in a way that brings the local and the global together.

2 How to provide a relevant and inclusive service to the significant number of young people who have migrated from other areas, people whose identity is tied up with a completely different culture when compared to the community in which they now live. Although there is a certain amount of homogeneity in global culture, there is also a significant diversity across local communities.

3 How to empower young people for whom access to modern technology and a growing array of commodities on which to spend their money may not necessarily equate with an increase in power. Unemployment, decreasing opportunities and increasing dependence on parents and/or social welfare are realities for a considerable number of young people in Ireland today, all of which may increase feelings of powerlessness.

4 How to address the fact that there are a considerable proportion of young people in the developing world who are living in abject poverty, slavery and war. For some of their communities, much of this misery, poverty and violence is caused by the demands of the large multinational companies for raw materials and for ever-cheaper labour to produce the commodities to meet the demands of young consumers in the West.

Youth work organizations are already addressing some of these issues, and notably in Ireland there is 'One World Week', a youth-led awareness-raising, education and action that takes place throughout Ireland annually, usually during November. It seeks to enable young people to learn about local and global justice issues, to make connections between the two and take action to bring about change. Past themes have been 'Images and Messages in Development' (2010); 'A Rich Man's World – Consume with Care' (2011) and 'Bouncing Back' (2012). Young people around the country vote on the theme that they feel should be covered. Another development in Ireland which has been covered elsewhere in this book (see Section 2, p. 83) is the establishment of Dáil na nÓg, which seeks to give young people a voice about matters that concern them.

At local level, youth workers can use modern technology to enable young people to produce film, exhibitions, drama and so on to add their voices to the dialogue about the world in which they live – local and global. In doing so, they will also have an opportunity to explore their own identity, culture and direction in a global world.

References, resources and further reading

Bourn, D., 2008, 'Young people, identity and living in a global society' in *Policy & Practice: A Development Education Review*, Vol. 7, Autumn 2008, pp. 48–61, available: http://www.developmenteducationreview.com/issue7-focus4. Accessed 19 June 2012.

Gidley, J., 2001, *Globalization and its Impact on Youth, Journal of Future Studies*, Vol. 6, No. 1, August 2001, pp. 89–106 available: *http://rmit.academia.edu/JenniferGidley/Papers/254927/Globalization_and_Its_Impact_on_Youth. Accessed 19.6.2012*

Information about 'One World Week' and back issues of the workshops and exercises are available from *www.youthdeved.ie* or *www.nyci.ie*

Further resources available at *www.developmenteducation.ie*

Donohoe, J. and F. Gaynor, 2007, *Education and Care in the Early Years*, 2nd ed., Dublin: Gill & Macmillan

Stiglitz, J., 2002, *Globalization and Its Discontents*, London: Penguin.

Tittley, M., 2009, *A New Approach to Youth Subculture Theory*. *http://sonlifeafrica.com/model/subcult3.htm*. Accessed 20 June 2012.

Cultural and SubCultural Influences on Consumer Behaviour, *http://crab.rutgers.edu*. Accessed 20 June 2012.

Hodgkinson, P., 2011, *Media Culture and Society*, London: Sage Publications.

Kahn, R. & Kellner, D., 2004, *Global youth culture*, http://www.gseis.ucla.edu/faculty/kellner/essays.html. Accessed 20 June 2012.

2

Understanding Youth Work

The History of Youth Work in Ireland

Legislation and Organisations

Purpose, Principles and Values

Volunteerism and Youth Work

The development of youth work as a profession is relatively new in Ireland but youth work itself has been going on for over a hundred years. This section aims to give a flavour of that development up to recent times, followed by a more in-depth description of legislative and policy and developments since the turn of the century.

Any attempt to capture the essence and ethos of a field as broad and complex as youth work in a book such as this is a challenge, so what is presented is a basic introduction to some of the ideals and ideas about the nature, purpose and approaches to youth work that have emerged over the years.

The History of Youth Work in Ireland

Early developments in youth work

Towards the end of the 1800s and in the early 1900s, concern about the morals of young people inspired a number of organisations and individuals to set up youth services and clubs. The defining characteristics of these were that they were mainly run by volunteers and had a strong religious and/or cultural influence.

At this time, Ireland was changing from a mainly agrarian society to one that was influenced by the industrial revolution, even if the industrial revolution itself did not hit Ireland to the same extent as elsewhere.

> Agrarian societies are based on agriculture, farming and working the land in rural areas.
>
> Industrial societies are based on factory and mechanical work, usually based in cities.

Irish Nationalism was also on the rise and the state was on the cusp of gaining independence. A number of the earliest youth organisations set up in Ireland were branches of British uniformed groups such as Boys and Girls Brigades (1893), the Boy Scouts (1908) and the Girl Guide movement (1911). A number of organisations instigated locally had strong cultural and nationalist leanings such as the Gaelic Athletic Association (1884), Inghindhe na hÉireann (1900) and Na Fianna Éireann (1913). These latter groups, while concerned with character-building for the young, were eager that young people be exposed to and learn to appreciate Irish language, history and games. The first Irish youth club, The Dublin Boys Club, was set up in 1911. Many of the early clubs had volunteers and funding from the St Vincent de Paul and the Legion of Mary.

The middle of the 1900s saw the development and expansion of these early beginnings; the post-war era was partly driven by concern for the large population of young and unemployed young men who were considered to be at grave risk of falling into moral decay. It was in the 1940s that the seeds of modern youth work as we know it in Ireland today was born. The then Archbishop of Dublin, John Charles McQuaid, along with the Department of Education requested that a youth welfare committee be established by the City of Dublin Vocational Education Committee (CDVEC). Thus Comhairle na Leas Óige was born (1942) with a statutory footing under the Vocational Educational Act 1930. This is now known as City of Dublin Youth Service Board (CDYSB). During this period other VECs throughout the country followed suit and supported the development of youth work services and committees to varying degrees and without any legal obligation or foundation. Crucially, this meant that these services were discretionary and depended on the commitment of local councillors and educationalists.

It was in the 1960s and 1970s that State support and intervention in youth work services took off in Ireland. This coincided with a period in which leisure time was growing and Irish youth was beginning to be influenced by a global youth culture (although the term had probably not yet been coined). On the one hand there was an explosion of pop music, and on the other there were the civil rights movements at home and abroad including a very strong student revolutionary movement. These decades also saw an increased interest and growth in psychological, social and behavioural theories. The abiding characteristic of youth work provision through all these developments has been the overwhelming voluntary contribution of all those directly involved on the ground.

The developments of this period included the establishment of National Youth Council of Ireland (NYCI) in 1968, the beginnings of the formation of Youth Policy at government level in establishing the O'Sullivan Committee in 1974 and the provision of the first grants for youth work in 1970.

 Activity:

Aim: To explore the development of youth work services and policy in a social and political context.

The first section of Table 2.2.1 is already filled in – brainstorm to complete the remainder. Complete column four using information from this chapter and from relevant websites listed at the end of the chapter.

Table 2.2.1 Development of youth work

Period	Social and political developments	Main concerns of youth work	Youth services and policies introduced
Late 1800s	Change from agriculture to industry Move of population to cities Democratic system of government Suffragette movement	Moral improvement of youth Good healthy sense of citizenship Limited access to education Slum dwelling and dangers of same	Boys' clubs Scouts GAA
1900–1930			
1940–1960			
1961–1980			
1981–2000			
2001–present			

This page may be photocopied.

Modern developments in youth work

While the overwhelming characteristic of youth work up to recent times was the voluntary nature of all those involved, the 1970s saw the beginnings of attempts to formulate a coherent government policy on youth and youth work. *A Policy for Youth and Sport* (1977) (the Bruton report) and *Development of Youth Work Services* (1980) (the O'Sullivan Committee report) laid the groundwork, but the Costello report, *The Final Report of the National Youth Policy Committee* (1984), proved to be a significant landmark in terms of the formulation of government youth policy. It proposed a structure for the delivery of a comprehensive youth service in Ireland, and many of its proposals were eventually reflected in the Youth Work Act 2001.

The Green Paper *Education for a Changing World* (1992) highlighted the need for an integrated approach to youth work provision and suggested a major role for the VECs. At the end of the same year a consultative group was established which included representatives from The National Youth Council of Ireland (NYCI), The National Youth Federation (NYF), Foróige, the VECs and the Department of Education and Science. The Green Paper together with the subsequent White Paper *Charting Our Education Future* (1995) paved the way for the first piece of legislation on youth work, the Youth Work Act 1997. Only one piece of the Act was implemented before a change of government occurred, but it was particularly important; the appointment of National Youth Work Advisory Committee (NYWAC). The new government promised amended legislation and this culminated in the Youth Work Act 2001.

The National Youth Advisory Committee (NYWAC) had an important role to play in preparing detailed guidelines for the implementation of the Act, which did not happen in any significant proportion until 2006.

While the governments were rewriting, revising and amending the legislation and legislative frameworks, the existing youth work organisations took full advantage of funding opportunities in the era of the Celtic Tiger. What developed, although undoubtedly positive, was uncoordinated, inconsistent and confusing, not least for the staff and volunteers trying to raise funds and deliver services. A single youth service could have funding from a variety of different sources and departments such as the Department of Education and Science; VECs; the Department of Justice, Equality and Law Reform; the Department of Tourism, Sport and Recreation; or the National Lottery.

Current funding schemes

The Youth Services Grant Scheme. The continued funding of major voluntary youth organisations both national and regional through this scheme is intended to ensure their continuance and development. Cutbacks mean that no new organisations will be considered for grants, but support of those already in the scheme will continue. This scheme is administered directly by the Department of Children and Youth Affairs.

Grants for Special Projects to Assist Disadvantaged Youths. Priority is given to 'out-of-school projects' in the spheres of special youth work initiatives, and those particularly aimed at young homeless people, young substance abusers and young travellers or in areas where there is a dense youth population and high unemployment.

Local Youth Club Grant Scheme: These grants are made available to youth clubs and groups through the local Vocational Education Committee. There are two types of grants, one for clubs and the other for activities.

Young People's Facilities and Services Fund: The objective of the fund is to assist in the development of youth facilities for 'at-risk' young people in disadvantaged areas to divert them away from substance abuse and crime, such as sporting and recreational facilities.

Youth Information Centre Grants Scheme: This is administered by the Vocational Education Committees on behalf Department of Children and Youth Affairs and aims to provide information on rights and opportunities on all levels to young people.

Policy papers and legislation

1977   *A Policy for Youth and Sport*: The Bruton Report

1980   *Development of Youth Work Services*: The O'Sullivan Committee Report

1984   *The Final Report of the National Youth Policy Committee*: The Costello Committee Report

1985   *In Partnership with Youth: The National Youth Policy*: Government's response to the Costello Committee Report

1992   *Education for a Changing World*: A Green Paper on Education

1993   *The Report of the Consultative Group on the Development of Youth Work*

1994   *Towards the Development of a Comprehensive Youth Service*: NYCI's policy document

1995   *Charting Our Education Future*: A White Paper on Education

1997   Youth Work Act

2000   National Children's Strategy

2001   National Children's Office

2001   Youth Work Act

2003   First Dáil na nÓg

2011   Department of Children and Youth Affairs established as a full and separate department

Young people's rights: young people's lives

The Irish State ratified the UN Convention on the Rights of the Child in 1990, and a number of key initiatives and developments have occurred since then. The government published the National Children's Strategy in 2000 and the National Children's Office in 2001, which had a principal function of implementing the strategy.

The strategy forms the kernel of Irish policy in relation to children and young people and has three primary goals:

1 Children will have a voice in matters which affect them.
2 Children's lives will be better understood; evaluation, research and information on their needs, rights and effectiveness of services for children will be instigated.
3 Children will receive quality supports and services to promote all aspects of their development.

(National Children's Strategy, 2000)

Children's Strategy Network

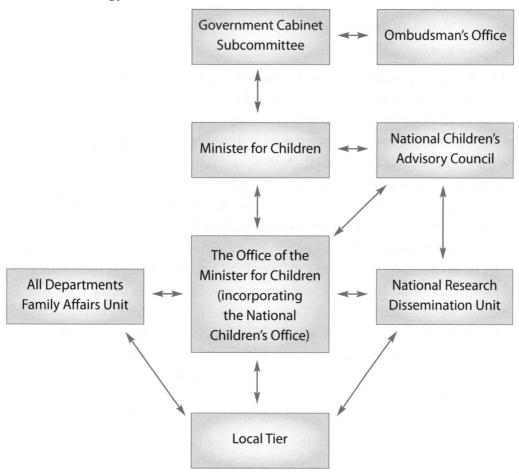

An initiative under the first goal of the strategy was the organising of **Dáil na nÓg** (Parliament of the Young). On a local level, Comhairle na nÓg allow 8- to 18-year-olds a forum for discussion. These local groups select representatives for an annual Dáil, which consists of 192 young people aged 12–18 drawn from various youth organizations and representing every county through the municipal comhairle in Ireland. Officials from relevant government bodies and non-governmental organisations (NGOs) also attend, and the government is usually represented by a minister. The National Youth Council of Ireland (NYCI) is currently responsible for the operation of this forum.

A further key element of the Children's Strategy was the creation of an **Ombudsman for Children**. A notable feature of the selection of the first ombudsman was the involvement of young people in the interview process; Emily Logan was duly appointed to the post in December 2003.

Recent developments

The growth of professionalism

The voluntary contribution of individuals in the field of youth work is huge and will hopefully continue to be so; according to NCYI, about 40,000 adult volunteers are involved in youth work currently. It is also recognised that youth work services must increasingly be of a high professional standard that requires training and education in order to engage in effective high quality intervention. An indication of the growing importance and development of the youth work sector was not only the employment of youth workers but also the advent of training courses and education. Some of the first professional youth workers in the 1970s in Ireland had been trained and educated on courses in Britain. Training in Youth and Community work began in Maynooth in the 1980s, and in 1990, the Department of Education supported those undertaking in-service professional training in the same college. Recently, FETAC offered the first Level 5 Certificate in Youth Work. The launch of both the North South Education and Training Standards Committee for Youth Work (NSETS) in 2006 and National Quality Standards Framework (NQSF) in 2010 set standards for both training of youth workers and quality of services.

North South Education and Training Standards Committee (NSETS)

Launched in 2006, NSETS saw the establishment of an all-Ireland professional endorsement framework for youth work education and training. However, as yet in the 26 counties there are no training requirements, or careers structures within the youth work sector; neither are there any set pay scales.

STATEMENT OF YOUTH WORK PRACTICE
Overview of National Quality Standards Framework

STATEMENT OF YOUTH WORK PRACTICE

What you do:	Why you do it:	Who is it for and with:	How you do it:	Where you do it:
ethos; mission; service provision; defining features/functions.	rationale; vision; aim and objectives; outcomes.	target group; partnerships; linkages; exchanges.	modes of provision; methodologies.	geographical area; settings; levels*; locations.

5 CORE PRINCIPLES All youth work practice and provision is:

1 Young-person-centred: recognising the rights of young people and holding as central their active and voluntary participation

Prescribed indicators
1.1 Systematic needs assessment.
1.2 Services responsive to the requirements of young people.
1.3 Services promote the strengths of young people.
1.4 Young people involved in the design, delivery and evaluation of services.
1.5 Clear examples of voluntary participation.

2 Committed to ensuring and promoting the safety and well-being of young people.

Prescribed indicators
2.1 Young people involved in the design, delivery and evaluation of services.
2.2 Clear examples of voluntary participation.
2.3 Health and safety policy and procedures.
2.4 Appropriate insurance cover.
2.5 Compliant with relevant legislation.

3 Educational and developmental.

Prescribed indicators
3.1 Theoretical and practical foundation.
3.2 Range of effective youth work methodologies.
3.3 Relevant and diverse programme/curriculum provision.
3.4 Evidence of planned and unplanned learning.
3.5 Developing personal and social

4 Committed to ensuring and promoting equality and inclusiveness in all its dealings with young people and adults.

Prescribed indicators
4.1 Accessible, inclusive and integrated services.
4.2 Policies, programmes and practices comply with equality legislation.
4.3 Policies, programmes and practices promote diversity, equality and inclusiveness.**

Capacities and competencies.

5 Dedicated to the provision of quality youth work and committed to continuous improvement.

Prescribed indicators
5.1 Culture and practice of innovation and critical reflection.
5.2 Service provision underpinned by principles of good practice.
5.3 Commitment to continuous development and quality assurance.
5.4 Commitment to resource effectiveness

Please identify one achieved outcome in relation to each of the core principles

Self-assessment and External Assessment	→	Continuous Improvement Plan	→	Progress Report

STANDARDS SECTION 1:
Youth Work Practice and Provision
1. Planning
2. Practice
3. Progression
4. Monitoring and Assessment
5. Policies and Procedures

STANDARDS SECTION 2:
Organisational Management and Development
1. Governance and Operational Management
2. Strategy
3. Volunteers
4. Human Resource Management
5. Collaboration and Integration

---

* The term 'levels' should be taken to mean the levels at which your organisation operates, e.g. local, regional, national or international.

** Equality and inclusiveness: The Equal Status Act 2000 prohibits discrimination on the following grounds: gender, marital status, family status, sexual orientation, religion, age (not including people under 18), disability, race (including colour, nationality and ethnic or national origin) and membership of the Traveller community.

National Quality Standards Framework (NQSF)

The National Quality Standards Framework (NQSF) is a support and development tool for the youth work sector which was launched in 2010. It provides a structured framework for organisations to assess, indicate and enhance their work. The standards outlined in the framework are intended to be reflective of the work being carried out in youth work organisations. Therefore, there should be both a commonality and compatibility between the current youth work provision of an organisation and its services, and the core principles and standards outlined in the NQSF.

– OMCYA, 2010, Summary of the National Quality Standards Framework, p. 1

Basically, the Framework sets out five core values and ten principles and standards against which youth work services will use to assess themselves within a three-year timeline. See chart on p. 85 for details.

National Youth Arts Programme (NYAP)

The National Youth Arts Programme is a partnership between the Youth Affairs Unit of the Department of Children and Youth Affairs, the Arts Council and the National Youth Council of Ireland (NYCI). The programme is delivered by the NYCI and is dedicated to the development and advancement of youth arts. It aims specifically to realise the potential of young people through good quality arts practice and to develop appropriate policies and activities at local, regional and national levels. Five key work areas are prioritised by the NYAP for its strategy for developing youth arts in Ireland:

- Advocacy (Policy and Practice)
- Networking
- Models of Practice and Related Issues
- Information and Resources
- Support and Development

National Youth Health Programme

The National Youth Health Programme is a partnership operated by the NYCI with the Youth Affairs Unit and the Health Promotion Unit of the Health Services Executive (HSE) respectively. The Programme aims to provide a broad-based, flexible health promotion/education support and training service to youth organisations and to all those working with young people in the non-formal education setting. This work is achieved through the development of programmes and interventions specifically for and with youth organisations throughout the country and the training and support of workers and volunteers implementing the programmes.

References, resources and further reading

Lalor, K., De Róiste, A. and M. Devlin, 2007, *Young People in Contemporary Ireland*, Dublin: Gill and Macmillan.

Devlin, M., 2012, *Youth Work Policy and Delivery*, Belfast: Youth Sector North South Working Group.

Jenkinson, H., 2000, 'Youth Work in Ireland: The Struggle for Identity' in *The Irish Journal of Applied Social Studies*, Volume 3/Issue 2. Article 6. Available at: *http://arrow.dit.ie/ijass/vol2/iss2/6*

The Office of Children and Youth Affairs *www.dcya.gov.ie*

The National Youth Council of Ireland *www.youth.ie*

Legislation and Organisations

Youth Work Act 2001

National Youth Work Development Plan 2003–2007

Youth work organisations

Youth Work Act 2001

Introduction

The Act, passed in December 2001, sets out on a statutory basis the framework for the provision of youth work in Ireland. It provides a definition of youth work and describes the functions of the Minister of Education and Skills and the VECs in this area and how they interact with youth work providers. The provisions of the Act become operable by ministerial order. A summary of the overall outline of youth work delivery envisaged by the Act, and of some of its key provisions, is provided below. Many of the provisions are not yet in operation.

Definitions

Youth work means 'a planned programme of education designed for the purpose of aiding and enhancing the personal and social development of young persons through their voluntary participation, and which is—

(a) complementary to their formal, academic or vocational education and training; and

(b) provided primarily by voluntary youth work organisations.'

A 'young person' is someone who is between the ages of 10 and 25.

National Youth Work Advisory Committee (NYWAC)

The NYWAC is appointed to advise and consult with the Minister on all youth work matters. It is composed of:

> Two or three ministerial nominees including the chairperson
> Two representatives from the Department of Education and Skills
> Eight representatives from other government areas
> Four representatives from the Irish Vocational Education Association

The *Prescribed National Representative Youth Work Organisation* nominates an equal number to all the above appointees excluding the chairperson (i.e. another 15 or 16 nominees). The Prescribed National Representative Youth Work Organisation is an organisation prescribed every three years by the Minister under the Act as representing voluntary youth work organisations. Currently the National Youth Council of Ireland is the prescribed organisation.

Local structures

The local Vocational Education Committees have a pivotal role in the framework outlined in the Act.

Voluntary Youth Council

Each Vocational Education Committee (VEC) area should have an elected Voluntary Youth Council to advise the VEC on preparing and implementing a Development Plan, to be a forum for voluntary youth work organisations operating in the area and to nominate persons to the area's Youth Work Committee. As far as possible, employees of youth work organisations shall not comprise more than 25% of Voluntary Youth Council's membership (i.e. at least 75% should be volunteers) and at least 20% should be young persons. The VEC will try to ensure that providers of youth work to Travellers are represented on the Council, and also providers of youth work in the Irish language if a Gaeltacht area is covered.

Youth Work Committee

Each VEC shall appoint a Youth Work Committee for its area to make recommendations on how the VEC performs its functions under the Act and to provide other advice as requested by the VEC. There will be from 16 to 20 members as decided by the VEC, half representing local relevant statutory agencies and half nominated by the area's Voluntary Youth Council.

Development Plans

Every three years each VEC must prepare a Development Plan for its area. The Plan shall specify the youth work requirements of the area and the measures needed to meet those requirements. In preparing each Plan, the VEC must consult with the area's Youth Work Committee and comply with any directions issued by the Minister including those requiring consultation with any specified persons or bodies.

The Plan must be submitted for approval to the Minister, who may amend it. It is deemed to be adopted when it is approved in writing by the Minister. A copy of the Plan must be available for inspection by the public at the VEC's head office.

Youth work functions of VEC

As far as is practicable, each VEC will ensure that youth work programmes and/or services are provided in its area by coordinating its plans with youth work organisations and providing assistance, including financial, to the organisations. It will endeavour to ensure coordination with education and other programmes for young persons in its area. The VEC will prepare a Development Plan as mentioned above and try to ensure all youth work in its area accords with the Plan.

Youth work functions of Minister

The Minister shall, as far as is possible, ensure the development and coordination of youth work policies, ensure the coordination of youth work programmes and services with education and other programmes provided to young persons, provide funds towards youth work, cause relevant research to be conducted, have regard to the information needs of young persons, monitor youth work programmes and services funded under the Act at least once a year and carry out an assessment at least once every three years of youth work provided by a recognised organisation in receipt of funds under the Act.

Assessor of Youth Work

The Minister may appoint an Assessor of Youth Work to exercise the Minister's monitoring and assessment functions who will provide an Annual Report of the Assessor to the Minister on the results of these assessments and any other matters the Minister may require. Regarding youth work programmes and services funded under the Act, the Assessor may examine their operation and any books/accounts relating to them, request any information required from the youth work provider and give the Minister and the provider a report of the examination. The Assessor has other functions relating to the interaction with, and recognition of, youth work organisations by the Minister and VECs.

Organisations

There are three types of organisations recognised under the Act that may receive financial assistance towards the provision of youth work. The Minister may in writing authorise as an *Authorised Organisation* any organisation which in his opinion 'engages from time to time in the provision of a youth work programme or service'. An *Approved National Voluntary Youth Work Organisation* is a voluntary youth work organisation that operates in two or more VEC areas and is approved in writing by the Minister. A VEC may designate in writing a voluntary youth work provider operating in its area as a *Designated Local Voluntary Youth Work Organisation* and will notify the Minister accordingly. A fourth type of recognised organisation is the Prescribed National Representative Youth Work Organisation. A list is published each year of all recognised organisations.

General

When carrying out their functions, and in drawing up Development Plans, the Minister and the VECs will have regard to equality of access and likely participation rates in youth work as between male and female young persons, the youth requirements of those who have attained age 10 but not age 21, those who are socially or economically disadvantaged and those who live in a Gaeltacht or whose first language is Irish.

Implementation

The NYWAC has been activated and has produced the National Youth Work Development Plan 2003–2007. A child protection sub-committee of the NYWAC has produced a Code of Good Practice for youth workers and has developed a training programme for relevant staff. Another sub-committee is working on the information needs of young persons. As mentioned above, the Prescribed National Representative Youth Work Organisation provisions have also become operable.

Current structure and funding*

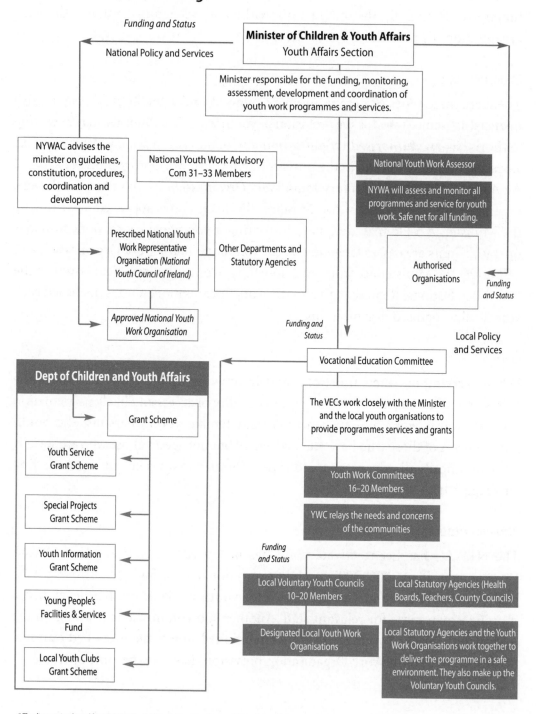

*The diagram is adapted from PJ Breen Youth Affairs Section, Department of Education and Science.

National Youth Work Development Plan 2003–2007

Although 2007 has been and gone and many of its recommendations have not been implemented, the National Youth Work Development Plan remains the blueprint for the development of youth work in Ireland.

The Plan was drawn up by the NYWAC following extensive consultations and a full review of existing youth work provision, and it is one of the major developments to flow from the enactment of the Youth Work Act 2001. A comprehensive document, it summarises the changing political, economic, cultural and international contexts for young people and youth work, with emphasis on social changes in the nature of youth itself and the impact of new information and communications technologies. The Plan provides a brief history of the development of Irish youth work policy and a summary of other policy initiatives in related areas such as social inclusion, combating disadvantage, health, child protection and children's rights, equality, education and EU developments.

The Plan sets out a strategy for the first five-year plan for the development of youth work in Ireland and is the first sustained examination of current youth services and their relationship with other aspects of youth policy and provision. It explores the challenges facing the youth work sector, depicts a vision of youth work in Ireland and sets goals and actions for the development of youth work over the next five years. The Plan aims to assist all young people to realise their full potential as individuals and to become active participants in a democratic society.

– Minister for Youth Affairs, Síle de Valera, 2003

The Plan specifies four goals to implement its vision for youth work and sets out over 40 specified actions to achieve those goals. The four broad goals agreed by the NYWAC are:

1. to facilitate young people and adults to participate more fully in, and to gain optimum benefit from, youth work programmes and services.
2. to enhance the contribution of youth work to social inclusion, social cohesion and active citizenship in a rapidly changing national and global context.
3. to put in place an expanded and enhanced infrastructure for development, support and coordination at national and local level.
4. to put in place mechanisms for enhancing professionalism and ensuring quality standards in youth work.

Of the specified actions, those identified as priorities were:

1 *The appointment of an Assessor of Youth Work.*

   This role was described under the terms of the Youth Work Act 2001, and the Plan also envisages the Assessor evaluating innovative youth work projects and ensuring the dissemination of learning from such projects.

2 *The creation of a Development Unit.*

   This national youth work Development Unit would have the over-arching objectives of researching and developing guidelines for best practice and assisting youth organisations to implement same; managing and coordinating research; piloting innovation; overseeing and monitoring the implementation of the relevant provisions of the Development Plan. Many of the specific action points set out in the Plan illustrate how the Unit would advance its remit – e.g. inviting proposals for new innovative projects by local or national youth organisations; researching how to further the social and political education, including the intercultural education, of young people, and how to promote citizenship and participatory democracy; promoting best practice on equality issues in youth organisations; developing structures for the active participation of young people in all aspects of youth work provision; establishing a charter of rights for young people in youth work and a charter for youth work volunteers; assisting youth groups and organisations to optimize their use of new information and communications technologies. Annex 1 to the Plan suggests models of how the Unit could be constituted.

3 *The establishment of a Funding Review Body.*

   The NYWAC should set up a Funding Review Body to ensure that funding of youth work is realistic; to identify staffing requirements and appropriate pay structures; to set criteria for the allocation of funding between and within schemes; to establish the rationale for determining the distribution of grant aid at national and area level; to develop benchmarks for the financial, human and capital resources required to ensure the continuation of quality youth work provision in a number of settings.

4 *The setting up of a Validation Body for Youth Work Training.*

A Youth Work Validation Body should be established to develop a comprehensive framework for accreditation and certification in youth work, in line with the provisions of the Qualifications (Education and Training) Act 1999 and allowing for accessible and flexible progression routes for both volunteers and paid workers. The Validation Body should represent all the relevant youth work interests in Ireland and should consider the comparable validation arrangements introduced in Northern Ireland.

5 *The expansion of the Local Youth Club Grants Scheme.*

The Local Youth Club Grant Scheme should provide additional support to local voluntary youth groups to ensure that adequate funding is made available as a direct support to the important youth work undertaken by volunteers in communities throughout the country.

A Children's and Young People's Policy Framework is currently in the process of completion; as part of this, the National Youth Policy Development Plan 2003–2007 is being reviewed.

Youth work organisations

As outlined earlier in the history of youth work, voluntary work and voluntary organisations have been central to the development and delivery of youth work services in Ireland and will continue to be so. Some of these are national organisations, some have specific interests, aims and objectives; their programme of activities reflect these. Below is a list of such organisations; it is not possible to include all those that exist in Ireland today, and also, it should be remembered that new programmes may be initiated, and old ones may change their names!

The National Youth Council of Ireland (NYCI)

Founded in 1967, NYCI is the representative body for national voluntary youth work organisations in Ireland and is recognised as such under the terms of the Youth Work Act 2001.

Aims of NCYI:

- to lead the way in raising the profile of the youth work sector
- to enhance the status of youth work and in particular, voluntary youth work
- to increase resources available to youth work
- to encourage interdependent relationships between member organisations

- to work in partnership with member organisations and encourage participation

Range of services includes:
- representation of its member organisations
- hosting a number of specialist and support programmes such as Youth Arts Programme, Youth Health Programme, Youth Development Education Programme, Child Protection Programme, International Programme, Intercultural and Equality Programme
- organising Dáil na nÓg in conjunction with DCYA
- advocating and lobbying on behalf of young people and the youth work sector in Ireland

For more information see *www.youth.ie*

Youth Work Ireland

Founded in 1962, Youth Work Ireland is a Federation of 22 local youth work services based throughout Ireland.

Aims of Youth Work Ireland:
- to co-ordinate and develop services
- to give voice to young people in these services
- to support and encourage both volunteers and staff
- to improve the quality of life for young people in the context of community-based services

Range of services includes:
- youth clubs and groups
- youth information centres
- after schools support groups
- work with early school-leavers
- community youth projects
- crime diversion projects
- international exchanges
- targeted youth initiatives and projects

For more information see *www.youthworkireland.ie*

Foróige

Founded in 1952 as Macra na Tuaithe, Foróige operates a national network of clubs and youth information centres throughout the 26 counties. It works in partnership and/or funded by VECs, Department of Justice and Law Reform, the Health Services Executive and Local Drug Task forces. In 2010 Ógra Chorcaí merged with Foróige.

Aims of Foróige:

- to enable young people to get actively involved
- to empower young people to make things happen
- to develop a youth education programme complementary to the home and school
- to provide learning experiences which foster personal development and enhances potential.

Range of services includes:

- Foróige youth clubs
- youth development programmes
- mentoring service
- youth cafés
- teen parent support programmes
- drug education and prevention programmes
- citizenship, health and well-being, and relationship and sexuality programmes
- partnership and fundraising for the Alan Kerins project in Zambia.

For more information see *www.foroige.ie*

Catholic Youth Care

Formerly the Catholic Youth Council, Catholic Youth Care was founded in 1944 and operates within the Dublin Catholic Archdiocese providing and supporting local youth work services in Dublin, Wicklow and parts of Kildare in partnership with some of the VECs.

Aims of Catholic Youth Care:

- to develop and support voluntary youth services with the Catholic Archdiocese of Dublin
- to provide direct services particularly in the most disadvantaged areas

- to promote social inclusion
- to commit to youth participation

Range of services includes:
- Garda Youth Diversion programmes
- drugs education
- local youth clubs
- adventure clubs
- youth information services
- summer projects
- outreach services
- youth worker and volunteer training

For more information see *www.cyc.ie*

BeLonGTo:

BeLonGTo is a national organisation for lesbian, gay, bisexual and transgendered (LGBT) young people aged between 14 and 23. Established in 2003, it has employed a full-time youth worker from the outset. It provides a direct youth service in Dublin and supports LGBT groups throughout the country. As well as providing a safe, relaxed, comfortable environment where LGBT young people can make friends with other young people in similar situations and find support, inclusion, acceptance and social justice, they also have the option of one-to-one support and access to information on education, health and legal services. In addition, BeLonGTo offers training to schools and other youth services and lobbies for social change.

For further information see *www.belongto.org*

Club4U

Club4U is a national organisation that arranges alcohol-free social events for young people. It also aims to educate them about the dangers of substance misuse. Furthermore, it aims to provide opportunities for the opinions of young people to be aired and heard nationally and internationally, and seeks to facilitate the promotion of peace, understanding and tolerance between young people and the communities in which they live. The organisation is supported by the Gardaí, the HSE and the Ombudsman for Children.

For further information see *www.club4u.ie*

The No Name Club

Founded in 1978, the No Name Club is also a national organisation similar in its aim to Club4U. It seeks to provide events and activities and opportunities to young people to enjoy themselves and develop in an atmosphere free of alcohol and drugs. It is supported by the DCYA and the HSE.

Youth Cafés

Youth Cafés have been set up all over the country by young people for young people in partnership with adults. They offer a relaxed alcohol- and drug-free environments where young people can come and go as they wish. Youth Cafés are often set up and run alongside other local youth work services. In 2010 the OMYCA produced a Toolkit that provided guidance on setting up a Youth Café. Also in recognition of the importance of such venues in the lives of young people and additionally, capital funding has been set to increase from €0.8m in 2011 to €1.5m in both 2012 and 2013.

> The Department of Children and Youth Affairs now estimates that between 75–100 youth café facilities now operate across the state and are seen as hugely beneficial to local communities in terms of broader engagement with young people. The projects are in many cases run directly by or in partnership with young people and are popular with teenagers and young people generally.
> – Frances Fitzgerald, Minister for Children and Youth Affairs on
> *www.dcya.ie* accessed 21 June 2012

Léargas

Léargas is the national agency in Ireland for the management of national and international exchange and cooperation programmes in education, youth and community work, and vocational education and training. It has been in existence for over 20 years and operates under the aegis of the Department of Education and Skills and the Office of the Minister for Children and Youth Affairs. There are opportunities and financial support for young people to travel to other countries as part of exchanges or to work on various projects, attend workshops and seminars over a wide range of topics and interests.

For more information see *www.leargas.ie*

SpunOut.ie

Spunout.ie was set up in 2004 and remains the only comprehensive online resource for youth health, lifestyle and citizenship. The website provides a host of information on youth health, information and activism. It contains listings of relevant civic events and opportunities and it also provides platforms for youth media, publishing, youth campaigns, advocacy and activism. The website is endorsed and supported by all the major agencies involved with youth in Ireland.

For much more information see *www.spunout.ie*

Uniformed organisations

These include Scouting Ireland, the Boys and Girls Brigades, The Irish Girl Guides and the Catholic Guides of Ireland.

Scouting Ireland

Scouting Ireland originated with the Boy Scouts, which was established in 1908. It is a part of the World Organisation of Scout Movement.

Scouting Ireland itself formed in 2004 as a result of merging Boy Scouts of Ireland and Catholic Scouts Ireland. Girls were first accepted in 1983 and are now involved at all levels.

The overall aim of Scouting Ireland is to provide programmes to promote the development of young people Socially, Physically, Intellectually, in their Character, Emotionally, Spiritually (the SPICES). This is to be achieved via the Scout Method, Personal Progress Awards and Programmes designed through the involvement of young people.

Range of services includes:

All the activities are delivered through 'One Programme' over six age groups or sections and include

- Activities and Challenges generally aimed at promoting responsibility and self-reliance
- Adventure Skills focussing on outdoor activities
- Special Interest Badges for which young people can develop special skills and interests
- Chief Scout Award, which can be linked to the An Gaisce Award.

For further information see *www.scouts.ie*

Council of Irish Guiding Associations

The Council of Irish Guiding Associations (Comhairle Bantreoraithe na hÉireann) was established in 1992 and was ratified as a full member of WAGGGS (World Association of Girl Guides and Girl Scouts) in 1992. The Council consists of the Irish Girl Guides and the Catholic Guides of Ireland.

The Irish Girl Guides and The Catholic Girl Guides

The Irish Girl Guides has been in existence since 1911. There are seven regions and four age groups.

The Catholic Girl Guides, founded in 1928. They are organised within each Catholic diocese and across four age groups, and cater for all denominations.

Both organisations are open to all young women and girls and aim to enable them develop their full potential through the provision of challenging programmes.

There is a strong emphasis on the outdoors, environment, community responsibility, teamwork and advocacy. Global issues and a sense of solidarity is fostered through association with WAGGGS.

For further information see *www.irishgirlguides.ie, www.girlguidesireland.ie* and *www.wagggsworld.org*

The Girls' Brigade and The Boys' Brigade

The Girls' Brigade and its fellow organisation **The Boys' Brigade** are international, Christian, uniformed youth organisations for girls and boys (respectively) of all ages, denominations, backgrounds and abilities. They were founded in 1893 and operate in 33 companies around the country across five age groups, offering a varied programme of activities designed to educate, challenge and inspire young people underpinned by a Christian ethos.

These uniformed organisations tend to train volunteers from within their ranks to become leaders.

For further information see *www.girlsbrigade.ie* and *www.boysbrigade.ie*

Young Men's Christian Association (YMCA) and Young Women's Christian Association (YWCA)

YMCA is a non-denominational worldwide movement that seeks to develop services and programmes to respond to the needs of young men. There is a wide range of programmes on offer that focus on outdoor education, vocational training, youth information, health education, homelessness, global youth work, peace and reconciliation and family youth work.

YWCA provides comparable opportunities for women, and particularly young women; the organisation also provides educational and recreational facilities and programmes to encourage all-round development. Both are broadly faith-based organisations.

Specialised groups

There are many other organisations and associations that provide outlets for young people but are usually tied to the specific aims of the particular organisation, for example:

- The *Gaelic Athletic Association (GAA)* focuses on development through sport, specifically Irish sports. The *Football Association of Ireland (FAI)* focuses on development through soccer.
- Youth branches of the various *political parties* encouraging citizenship and activism and tied to the political party's specific aims and agendas.
- *Union of Students in Ireland (USIT)* provides information, services and a lobbying platform for students in Ireland.
- *Macra na Feirme* is located mainly in rural Ireland and its clubs encourage involvement in a number of areas including agriculture, sports, travel, public speaking, performing arts and community involvement.
- *Eco-UNESCO* aims to develop and channel the energies of young people into positive and creative actions to protect the environment.
- *Amnesty International* promotes the protection of human rights throughout the world and has a youth section through which young people can become active in defending human rights at home and abroad.

References, resources and further reading

Department of Education and Science, 2003, *National Youth Work Development Plan 2003–2007*. Dublin: Stationery Office.
The Youth Work Act 2001, Dublin: Stationery Office.
Department of Children and Youth Affairs www.dcya.gov.ie
See the full list of members of the NYCI at www.youth.ie

Purpose, Principles and Values

What is youth work?
The nature of youth work
The purpose of youth work
The ethos or values underpinning youth work
Youth work methods

What is youth work?

The Youth Work Act (2001) clearly defines youth work as a planned programme of education designed for the purpose of aiding and enhancing the personal and social development of young persons through their voluntary participation, which is complementary to their formal, academic or vocational education and training and provided primarily by voluntary youth work organisations. Youth work is particularly aimed at young people aged ten to 25 years, and focuses on the holistic development of a young person. The strategically planned programmes of education are specifically focused at meeting the needs of young people and offer diverse means of education. The young people's active participation in the programmes is vital for each participant to reach their full potential. It is important to realise that there are other service providers (such as social workers, the Gardaí or career guidance counsellors) and other networks within young people's communities and among their peer groups with which young people have contact and which also have a bearing on their overall development.

The nature of youth work

The UN Convention on the Rights of the Child, Article 12, upholds the right of the young person to voice their opinion, have their views listened to and be taken seriously. There are essential features that determine how youth work is to be delivered if a youth service is committed to this principle, so any youth service must be based upon:

- Voluntary participation: each person must come to the youth service of their own free will. They have a choice to participate in activities run by the centre.
- Youth-centred approach: The youth service's approach should be holistic and centred on the youth; it should be all about the young person. The NYCI

suggests starting 'where young people are at'. The approach should be flexible enough to accommodate all young people's interests and abilities.

- Partnerships: two-way communication must play a vital role in order to build relationships within the group. Opportunities for real involvement in decision-making and taking responsibility should be provided.

The purpose of youth work

- to offer praise and encouragement to young people
- to enable young people to make choices and accept consequences
- to assist young people with conflict resolution among their peers and other adults
- to enable young people to realise their full potential
- to introduce young people to new experiences
- to provide appropriate challenges for young people and facilitate the skills they need to overcome them
- to manage young people's self-esteem and self-confidence and use it productively
- to enable young people to develop social awareness and a sense of social solidarity
- to develop a world view of issues that affect young people's lives
- to enable young people to have a voice and a place in their communities where they are listened to
- to work with other agencies with a view to to encouraging the whole of society to be responsive to young people's needs
- to improve young people's role as active citizens

 Activity:

List some activities that the youth worker could plan with a group of young people to show that most activities, planned or unplanned, will encapsulate the purposes of youth work. Complete the exercise on p. 105 on planning a bag-packing fundraiser by matching the activities on the left with the purposes of youth work on the right. Next, create a similar matching game with different activities. For example, playing pool in youth services, having art and craft classes, etc. This exercise can be done alone or in groups.

Matching game

Research a charity	Improve young people's role as active citizens
Choose a charity and contact to inform them of your fundraiser	Offer praise and encouragement to young people
Contact business people	Enable young people make choices and accept consequences
At local level ask for support	Assist young people with conflict resolution among their peers and other adults
Approach a local supermarket	Enable young people to realise their full potential
Appoint a coordinator fairly	
Decide on a campaign slogan	Introduce young people to new experiences
Print posters and flyers	Provide appropriate challenges for young people and facilitate the skills they need to overcome them
Get buckets and cover with charity information	
Devise a rota of people for bag-packing	Manage young people's self-esteem and self-confidence and use it productively
Pack the bags	Enable young people to develop social awareness and a sense of social solidarity
Count money donated	
Go to bank and lodge using appropriate forms	Develop a world view of issues that affect young people's lives
Evaluate the activity	Enable young people to have a voice and a place in their communities where they are listened to
Give feedback to local community	
Send thank-you notes	Work with other agencies with a view to encouraging the whole of society to be responsive to young people's needs

The ethos or values underpinning youth work

The following values should underpin and be reflected in the policy of any committed, high-quality youth service:

- respect for the young person as a unique individual with rights and needs
- commitment to an environment that is based on mutual trust, honesty and openness
- commitment to the principles of equality of access and participation
- valuing diversity and a commitment to the provision of an environment that is free from prejudice and discrimination
- a commitment to the empowerment of all young people by imparting the knowledge and skills to enable them to take responsibility in their own lives.
- a genuine democratic approach that shares power and decision-making with the young people
- a commitment to advocacy; enabling and supporting young people in identifying their needs and entitlements and in accessing services. Also, a commitment to highlighting these and lobbying with young people and on their behalf.

Youth work methods

Youth work is about the provision of planned non-formal education. The methods that the services use will depend on the areas of education being focused on. In view of the fact that youth work is based on voluntary participation, it is important that a variety of methods be used to suit all styles of learning, to maintain interest and to encourage interactive learning. The exploration of diverse areas of education is necessary to promote the holistic development of the young person.

Planning the youth work curriculum involves identifying the area of education, choosing an approach to this area and devising activities using appropriate methods of implementation. See examples on the following pages.

Table 2.3.1 Youth work methods by areas of education

Areas of education	Approach through	Example
Recreational	Any outdoor or sporting pursuits	Ball games, athletics, hill walking, water sports
Creative .	Drama, music, art, theatre	Song, dance, acting, painting, pottery
Justice and spiritual	Legal or faith education and development	Religious topics, law and order, consumer rights
Issue-based information	Any topics based on equality, political or environmental issues	Recycling, environmental awareness, democracy
Social media	Using social media as a communicative tool	Information on using social networking sites highlighting the advantages and disadvantages, learning how to use technology positively
Intercultural and international awareness	Youth exchanges and voluntary international services	Student exchange programmes or celebrating different cultures, volunteering with Goal or Concern
Welfare	Any health or well-being initiatives, life skills and teamwork	Health promotion, substance awareness, sexual health, first aid, relationships, bullying

All of these are achieved by methods such as:

- individual reflection
- small group discussion
- large group discussion and debate
- role play exercise
- creating a visual-art-, drama- or music-based presentation
- preparing and delivering a group presentation
- playing interactive games
- providing feedback from discussions and activities
- participating in experiential learning exercises
- participating in teamwork activities
- completing written questionnaires and activity sheets and quizzes
- singing competitions, dance workshops,
- interactive training programmes
- active, co-operative and experiential learning
- peer education programmes

 Activity:

Using the template overleaf, choose an area of education and an approach through which the area can be developed. Give an example of an activity and choose some methods you could use to deliver the programme.

Area of Education	
Approach	
Example	
Methods	

Some of the methods mentioned here are dealt with in greater detail elsewhere in the book, such as peer education, reflective practice, and also a section on equality and diversity. There are excellent resources out there for youth workers to choose from, and with each youth service being different and based on different models of youth work practice, it is important to get what is most suitable for the setting you are working in.

Volunteerism and Youth Work

Volunteering in youth work

Historically the work of volunteers has been at the core of youth work in Ireland, and all of the earliest youth clubs and organisations were voluntary: Guides, Scouts, Brigades, etc. Today youth work services on the ground have an overarching voluntary dimension. It is because of voluntary work that youth work exists in its present form. This is clearly recognised both in the Youth Work Act 2001 and National Youth Work Development Plan. A key element of the Youth Work Act is that it recognises voluntary organisations as the primary providers of youth work.

There are three dimensions to volunteerism in youth work according to Devlin (2009) relating to i) young people, ii) adults and iii) the organisations.

The purpose of this section is look at the second dimension, the adult volunteer, in order to give a broader understanding of volunteerism, including:

- the definition of a volunteer
- reasons why people volunteer
- different types of volunteers
- policies, procedures and guidelines for selection, recruitment, training and on-going support of volunteers

What is a volunteer?

A volunteer is somebody who gives up their time, skills, and talents freely to help a cause or other people without expecting or receiving any pay. This may be anything from helping at a children's hospital on a weekly basis to clearing up rubbish in your estate twice a year.

Participants at the National Consultation Seminar on Volunteering in the Youth Sector (2007) came up with some definitions that give an idea of the different levels at which volunteering in youth services may take place.

> 'Volunteering is giving up your time and expertise/experience freely to influence and shape the development of young people, volunteers and youth organisations at local/regional/national level.' (p. 5)

> 'A volunteer is someone who gives up their time for others' reward because they care about their communities and people, are motivated to help other people, while being outgoing and willing to do stuff.' (p. 5)

People volunteer for a great variety of reasons. Some people do it as a natural part of their involvement with their friends, neighbours and community on an ad hoc basis. Examples of this might be passing on information in the neighbourhood, picking up shopping for a friend who has just had a baby or giving lifts to members of a team going to play a match.

Others volunteer because they have a passion for an activity or interest, such as coaching in the local hurling club, helping with an environmental conservation project, or recovering drug addicts doing talks in schools and youth services.

Still others volunteer because they 'want to give something back'. This might be typical of a considerable number of volunteers in youth work organisations; they have had some wonderful experiences of growing up as part of a club, and want to be involved in giving the next generation the same opportunities.

There is also a growing number of retired people who have years of experience and specific talents which can be put to good use by volunteering, like retired teachers giving adult literacy classes or a retired accountant doing the books for the local youth club.

Someone may start off packing bags in a supermarket to raise much-needed funds for a club and may end up taking charge of weekly activities. The limitations to voluntary work are endless in this regard.

Although there is no financial reward for voluntary work and it is largely done from a sense of altruism, there are guaranteed outcomes for the volunteer; a growth in self-esteem and self-confidence, a sense of achievement, pride, and most importantly, enjoyment.

> Altruism means selfless concern for others and their welfare.

 Activity:

Brainstorm all the types of voluntary work and workers you can think of.
    List things that you yourself have done. Think about why you did it and what the reward was for you, if any, in doing it.

Types of volunteer

The Working Group on Volunteering (2007) distinguished between different types of volunteer in the youth sector:

Table 2.4.1 Types of volunteer

Type	Description	Example
Occasional	Volunteer at short-term events or offer specific skills to projects	Summer camps/art projects Accountancy/gardening
Regular	Volunteer on an ongoing basis. Their contribution supports and compliments that of the staff	At football matches every week
Specific	Volunteer for specific tasks because of their skills, knowledge and experience	Security, or the young people's representative on the board of management
Young	Can volunteer in any of the areas mentioned, but are particularly useful volunteers in Peer education.	Dáil na nÓg or peer mentors

It is possible for all different types of volunteers to overlap in all areas of organisations. Therefore careful planning is required to make optimum use of time and talents.

Policies and procedures

'A key challenge for youth service managers … is to develop recruitment, induction and retention policies aimed at volunteers which seeks to harness the natural enthusiasm of volunteers in a focused and manageable manner' (Hurley, 1993, p. 49). Every organisation should have policies and procedures in all areas related to volunteers. These policies should put structure on volunteering in organisations and provide clear procedures for all staff whether voluntary or paid. They should be transparent and made available to all members of staff. If possible all members (including current volunteers) of the youth service should be involved in the policy making.

The main areas to be covered are:
- Recruitment and selection
- Induction and training
- Ongoing support

Recruitment and selection

Policy and procedures should include answers to the following:
- Who is ultimately responsible for the recruitment of volunteers?
- What and who should be involved in the decision-making process?
- Where should the interviews take place?
- If shortlisting applies, what will this process be?
- How are applicants informed after interview?
- What background checks are required? (Garda clearance, references, etc.)
- What other issues need to be considered? (Health and safety, insurance cover, etc.)

A checklist can be used to standardise procedures, noting things like experience, references, interests, hobbies, etc.

Induction and training

When volunteers start up they will settle in more quickly and confidently if they know their way around, have been introduced to at least some of the other workers and are clear about roles, responsibilities and boundaries. All this does not happen naturally and needs careful thought and planning.

Policies and procedures should consider the following:
- When and how does induction take place?
- Who is responsible for ensuring that all volunteers are inducted and trained?
- What budget is available for induction and training?
- An outline of the role and responsibilities of the volunteer.
- Clear guidelines on confidentiality, access to and exchange of information.
- A clear introduction to reporting and recording procedures.

Again, a checklist should be drawn up so that nothing is overlooked in the induction of any volunteer.

Ongoing support

Once the volunteer is selected, supervision and support is imperative to the retention of the volunteers, their energy and enthusiasm, and also to help with the smooth running of the centre. This involves regular meetings with the volunteers to address general concerns and deeper issues if needs be. The facilitator must inform the volunteer of all positive and negative aspects of their work as an integral part of these meetings, keeping in mind that praise and encouragement improves everyone's morale. Goals need to be set and reviewed so that the volunteer can see the effect of their contribution in a very concrete way.

Policies and procedures could take account of the following:
- Who is responsible for ongoing supervision and support?
- When is it carried out – weekly, monthly or at the end of every session?
- How does the supervisor show that the organisation values the contribution of the volunteer?
- How are shortcomings/mistakes/complaints to be handled?
- Confidentiality during all supervision and support meetings must be observed by all parties
- A written record of the meeting must be taken and signed by both parties.

Starting Out: A National Induction Training Programme for Volunteers Engaged in Youth Work Practice is an invaluable resource for all youth workers. The resource contains a variety of worksheets, factsheets and accompanying PowerPoint slides, which can be downloaded from www.youth.ie/startingout and used as required. The factsheets provide information in relation to each of the components in the programme. The worksheets contain exercises which can be used either on a one-to-one basis or in a group context in order to facilitate experiential learning, discussion and application of the components to youth work practice.

It is important to remember that this induction programme focuses on supporting volunteers to achieve a set of learning outcomes included in each component, bearing in mind that organisations may wish to add additional learning outcomes as per their own induction training programmes.

For more information on volunteers please see resources below.

References, resources and further reading

National Youth Council of Ireland *www.youth.ie*
Volunteering Ireland *www.volunteeringireland.com*
Comhairle *www.comhairle.ie*
Volunteer Now (NI) *www.volunteering-ni.org*
Volunteer Centres Ireland *www.volunteer.ie*

CYDSB, 2009, *A Guide to Developing Policy on Volunteering in Essential Guidelines for Good Youth Work Practice Toolkit.*
Human Resource Solutions, 2012, Induction Policies/Induction Checklists at http://www.human-resource-solutions.co.uk. Accessed 22 June 2012.
Monaghan, L. and McGrory, S., 2010, *Starting Out: A National Induction Training Programme for Volunteers engaged in Youth Work Practice.* Dublin: NYCI.
National Youth Council of Ireland, 2007, *Resource on Volunteering and Volunteer Support in the Youth Sector.* Dublin: NYCI.

3

Working with Young People

Processes and Social Learning

Participation

Working with Groups

Reflective Practice

Peer Education

Good Practice Guidelines

Health and Safety

Child Protection

This section focuses on the factors, skills, interactions and processes involved in working directly with young people. It is important to consider the factors that affect the daily lives of the young people who attend, but it is also important to understand the processes of learning, group work, leadership and peer education. This understanding in turn enables the youth workers to appraise their own performance and ways of working, and therefore to improve constantly. The youth workers have serious and onerous responsibilities and duties of care to those young people with whom they work, so the latter part of the section is devoted to best practice guidelines in general, but also in relation to health and safety issues, and last but by no means least, to child protection.

Processes and Social Learning

Factors that shape young people's lives
The process of learning in youth work
The learning cycle
Types of learning
Learning styles

It is important as a youth worker to seek to understand what is relevant and important in a young person's life. Through this examination you will fulfil one of the purposes of youth work: to start from 'where the young person is at'.

Factors that shape young people's lives

 Activity:

There are two strands to this activity. Look at the illustration on the next page and examine the various factors that affect our everyday lives.

In the first column, write down the things that are important in your life.

In the second column, write down the things that you think a young person would prioritise.

Priorities for you in your life	The things that you think a young person would prioritise

Extension of this activity:

Photocopy the illustration and bring it to the youth service. Organise an activity based on thinking about what factors shape young people's lives and why. Use the illustration with the group and ask them to write a list from 1 to 10, numbering 1 as most important and numbering 10 as the least important.

Think about the differences, if any, between the young person's list and yours.

The information from this exercise can help you to empathise with the group and understand them better. It also helps in planning activities.

The process of learning in youth work

It is imperative that youth workers understand how young people learn. An American educational theorist, David A. Kolb, believed that 'learning is the process whereby knowledge is created through the transformation of experience' (1984, p. 38). Kolb's theory of learning is built upon earlier work by two other well-known theorists, John Dewey and Kurt Lewin. The theory is a cyclical model of learning, consisting of the four stages listed below. Real learning may occur at any stage of this cycle, but the learning must follow the sequence of the cycle. This is similar to Piaget's developmental stage theory of cognitive development. Piaget believed that a person must complete each stage sequentially before moving on to the next.

The learning cycle

The four stages of the learning cycle are

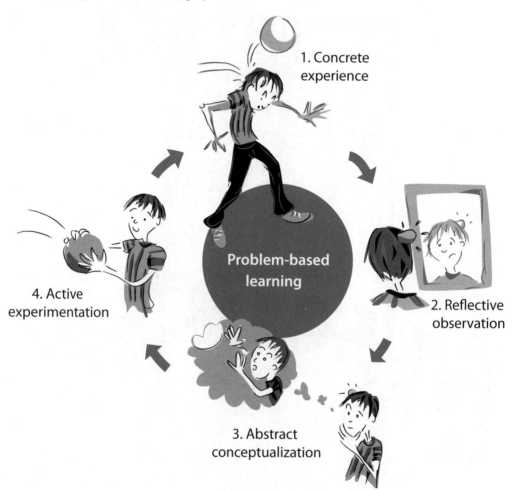

1. Concrete experience

2. Reflective observation

3. Abstract conceptualization

4. Active experimentation

Problem-based learning

Table 3.1.1 The four stages of the learning cycle

Concrete experience	Getting hit on the head with the ball.
Reflective observation	'I hate getting hit on the head. It's sore.'
Abstract conceptualisation	'They are always throwing balls at my head and laughing when they hit me. What if I catch the ball and throw it back?'
Active experimentation	Starts practicing throwing and catching the ball. One day, he throws it back. He feels great.

 Activity:

One Monday evening in the youth club, the girls are having a pampering evening, which involves manicures, make-up application and hair styling. The youth worker is present in a supportive role. The girls, however, are managing the time, resources, etc., themselves.

It is all going well until Katie arrives, late, and is not aware that a pampering evening was planned, as she was not present last Monday. Katie is annoyed, and starts shouting at the girls. Tina retaliates, leading to a screaming match between the two of them, and the potential for violence emerges.

The youth worker intervenes.

Katie and Tina are separated.

The youth worker speaks to both of them separately, and after some reflection, they all talk together.

Katie says that this is typical of the other girls' behaviour, that they're always planning things without her. She thinks that they should know that she would hate a pampering evening.

Tina says this is exactly what she would have expected from Katie, who only attends the club sporadically and then expects the group to choose activities that she likes to do.

Both are frustrated.

When the youth worker facilitates a discussion between the two girls, all is revealed and they feel a lot better about the situation.

Katie confides that she has a lot going on at home and feels that nobody ever listens to or understands her. She is working part-time to help her mum pay the bills and is exhausted most of the time.

Tina has a lot going on at home too, as there is a lot of pressure on her from her parents about her school work. She needed a break from study and just wanted an evening of pampering.

Both Katie and Tina have now gone through the first three stages of the educational learning cycle.

Write what you think might happen at stage four:

_____

_____

_____

_____

_____

_____

_____

_____

The youth worker's role on this occasion was to

- facilitate discussion between the two girls
- identify aspects of their behaviour that was not acceptable
- realise the implications that their behaviour had on the rest of the group
- encourage both girls to reflect on what happened and think about how they can change their behaviour so this will not happen again

This is all done through talking, reflecting and understanding.

How to you think the youth worker's intervention helped this situation?

_____

_____

_____

_____

_____

Types of learning

There are three different types of learning in group settings:

Formal learning is typically in a classroom environment and is highly structured, for example, in school.

Non-formal learning is planned learning that takes place out of the school context, for example, at a youth centre.

Informal learning refers to incidental learning that takes place through everyday encounters with people, for example, going to the park with your friends.

Out of the three types of learning, informal is the most common and the best form of active learning, and is also known as experiential learning. Experiential learning has been described as:

> Tell me and I may forget
> Show me and I may remember
> Involve me and I will understand
> – Anon.

Learning styles

There are different approaches to learning because all people learn differently. There are three styles of learners: visual, auditory and kinaesthetic.

■ Visual learners, who learn through the use of visual aids. They usually prefer to see the instructor and watch their non-verbal communication. Diagrams, flipcharts, videos, books with illustrations and slide shows are all methods of learning that visual learners prefer.

■ Auditory learners find listening to others easier than reading text. Group work, discussions and recordings are very useful for this method of learning. The auditory learners are often very good at interpreting other people's tone of voice, speed and pitch.

■ Kinaesthetic learners learn best with a hands-on or tactile approach. Structured learning would be very difficult for this type of learner, and their preference is for actively exploring the physical world around them.

In summary, youth work is a mixture of non-formal and incidental learning involving young people with all different learning styles. It is important for youth workers to realise that in order to meet young people's needs to grow and develop, their learning styles must be identified early on and taken into consideration when planning activities. See resources below to find learning style surveys to carry out with your group.

References, resources and further reading

Kolb, David A., 1984, *Experiential Learning: Experience as the Source of Learning and Development.* Prentice-Hall: Englewood Cliffs, NJ.

To identify your learning style, go to:
http://www.howtolearn.com
http://people.usd.edu/~bwjames/tut/learning-style/

Participation

What is participation?
Ladders of participation
Beginning the participation process
Promoting an effective youth–adult partnership
The youth worker's role in youth participation

What is participation?

Participation is often referred to as the 'process of sharing decisions which affect one's life and the life of the community in which one lives' (Hart, 1992, p. 5).

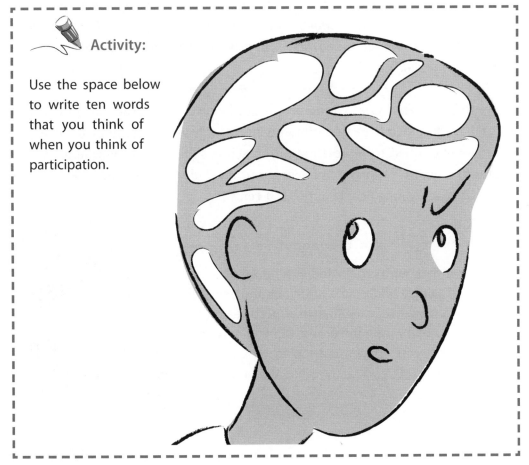

Activity:

Use the space below to write ten words that you think of when you think of participation.

There are two articles in the UN Convention on the Rights of the Child that give leverage to the notion that children and young adults should have a say in matters affecting their lives. The notion of participating in decision-making is very much to the fore of this process.

Article 12 of the Convention states:

> *States' Parties shall assure to the child who is capable of forming his or her own views the right to express those views freely in all matters affecting the child, the views being given due weight in accordance with the age and maturity of the child [and] for this purpose the child shall, in particular, be provided with the opportunity to be heard in any judicial and administrative procedures affecting the child.*

Article 13 of the Convention states:

> *The child shall have the right to freedom of expression; this right shall include freedom to seek, receive, and impart information and ideas of all kinds, regardless of frontiers, either orally, in writing or in print, in the form of art, or any other media of the child's choice.*

Currently, more and more young people are involved in decision-making about things that affect their lives: there are student councils in many schools and colleges; students are entitled to representation on schools' boards of management; and classroom rules are decided more democratically. This trend is a positive move for the children and young people of the 21st century.

Think about...

... a time that you participated in a group activity or event. For example, being a bridesmaid, sitting on the debs committee, joining the scouts, becoming a member of a sports team. Reflect on how much control you had within the group. Did you make decisions, were you allowed voice your opinion, did your actions change anything? Did you feel listened to? Were you actively or passively involved? What could have improved things?

Sherry Arnstein (1969), in exploring participation and democracy in the US, developed an eight-step 'ladder of participation'; each step represents the level of control that a person has over an initiative, i.e. what is happening.

Ladders of participation

8 Citizen control
7 Delegated power
6 Partnership
5 Placation
4 Consultation
3 Informing
2 Therapy
1 Manipulation

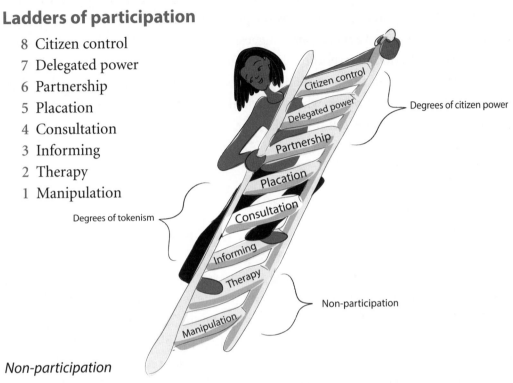

Non-participation

1 Manipulation
2 Therapy

These two rungs of the Ladder of Participation denote informing young people in a non-participatory way. On these lowest two steps, the person is told what to do and informed about what is happening; they are not involved in any way in the decision. This may be the part of the initial process when a young person first joins the youth service. They are participating because they have willingly joined the club. The leader 'knows best', and will instruct the participants in the basic rules of the club, for example, subs to pay, location of fire exits, etc.

Degrees of tokenism

3 Informing
4 Consultation
5 Placation

The next three steps move from minimal participation to being involved in the decisions being made. Informing (3) is a bit like an induction for the young people, and is usually a one-way communication. On the next rung, consultation (4) occurs and participants are asked their views. This is sometimes when the group rules are devised, decided upon and adopted by the group. Placation (5) occurs when people in the group start to make meaningful suggestions, but ultimately the power remains with the youth leader. Discretion is key to successful placation, and youth leaders have to balance out all the personalities and various needs that are at stake. They must pacify the participants while still making decisions on the strength and practicality of the notions put forward.

Degrees of citizen power

6 Partnership
7 Delegated Power
8 Citizen Control

The last three rungs are reached when the power is being shared, delegated and ultimately handed over. At this level, young people who have successfully climbed each rung of the ladder have a say in decision-making. As a result, they may be on the board of management, or represent the young people of the youth service on other levels, or for example by lobbying for more resources for the youth centre. Eventually the young person could even study youth work or other disciplines related to this field of work, become qualified and may become the manager of the youth service.

Shier, (2001) offered a useful alternative to Arnstein's Ladder of Participation. The Pathways to Participation model consists of five levels of participation. At each level, individuals and organisations have different degrees of commitment to the process of empowerment, i.e. giving power. The model tries to clarify this by identifying three stages of commitment at each level: Openings, Opportunities and Obligations.

Table 3.2.1 Shier's (2001) Pathways to Participation

Levels of Participation	Openings	Opportunities	Obligations
5. Children share power and responsibilities for decision-making.	Are you ready to share power with children?	Is there a procedure that enables children and adults to share power and responsibility for decisions?	Is it a policy requirement that children and adults share power and responsibility for decisions?
4. Children are involved in decision-making processes.	Are you ready to let children join in your decision-making processes?	Is there a procedure that enables children to join in the decision-making processes?	Is it a policy requirement that children be involved in decision-making processes?

This point is the minimum you must achieve if you endorse the UN Convention on the Rights of the Child.

3. Children's views are taken into account.	Are you ready to take children's views into account?	Does your decision-making process enable you to take children's views into account?	Is it a policy requirement that children's views must be given due weight in decision-making?
2. Children are supported in expressing their views.	Are you ready to support children in expressing their views?	Do you have a range of ideas and activities to help children to express their views?	Is it a policy requirement that children must be supported in expressing their views?
1. Children are listened to. **START HERE**	Are you ready to listen to children?	Do you work in a way that enables you to listen to children?	Is it a policy requirement that children must be listened to?

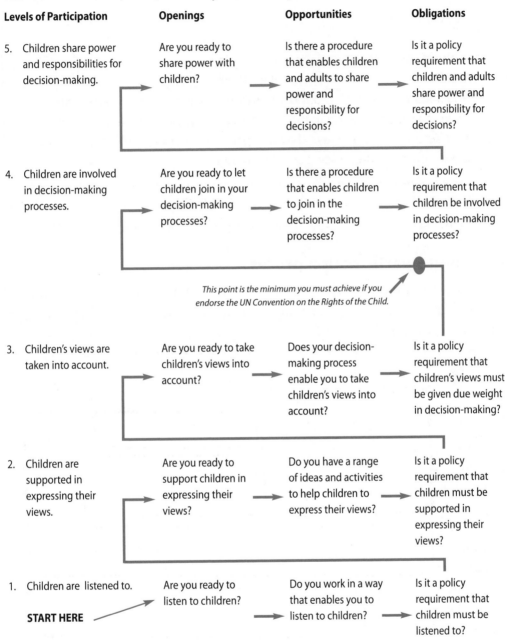

Adapted from Shier, H., 2001, 'Pathways to participation: Openings, opportunities and obligations', *Children and Society.*

Activity:

Think about the youth service you are working in.

What kind of participation takes place there?

Who initiates it, and what opportunities are given for overall participation?

Using the Ladder of Participation or the Pathways of Participation, depending on your setting, identify ways that the youth worker can facilitate the young person to complete the process of participation.

In the *Youth Participation Resource Pack* there is an excellent template on page 27 that all youth services can use. You can find this resource pack online www.youth.ie.

Beginning a participation process

Participation and youth–adult partnerships don't just happen; these processes must be initiated and be fostered over a long period of time with a lot of effort on the part of the youth service.

Activity:

In the space to the right brainstorm all the factors that you consider important in initiating a youth–adult partnership.

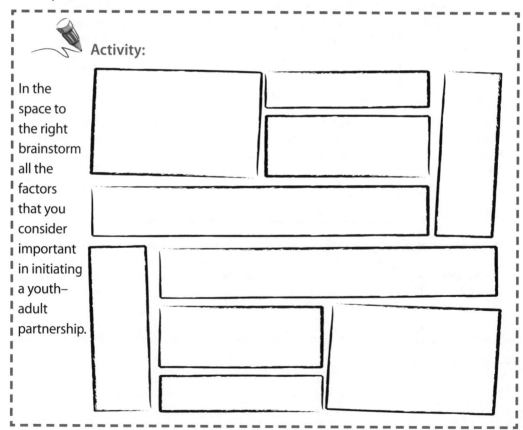

The following must be considered before an effective youth–adult partnership can evolve.

Understanding of power and ability

Young people need to realise that the youth worker is in a position of control and can therefore decide how much or how little control to allow others. If the youth worker decides to give over some control, the young people need to show their ability to use this power sensibly and to mutual benefit. Power is dependent on information, confidence, skill and money. If the young people have no power or say in decision-making processes, they are not partners in the youth–adult partnership.

Stakeholders

Youth workers have to think about the different stakeholders involved and what they have to lose or gain by looking at the overall set-up of the youth service. Questions need to be answered such as:

- Who will be affected by the project?
- Who controls the money to finance different ventures?
- Who has the information and skills necessary to complete the project?

Commitment

When people want to achieve something, they are usually committed. If people have a stake in a project, they tend to care more about it. For example, if the young people respect the game consoles, they may have care more about the games room. Apathy or lack of interest is relative to the stake people have in ideas, projects and outcomes. The less involved they are, the less commitment they will give to the venture.

Opportunities to develop

Young people cannot be expected to make ground-breaking decisions from the start. This process involves lots of support for the young people and opportunities to develop confidence by being given lighter responsibilities at first. This is part of climbing the ladder; young people are encouraged to make decisions, but at each stage they have the support of the youth workers in a controlled environment.

Training

Young people may need training in communication, decision-making, leadership and teamwork skills. It is important not to let young people put themselves in situations for which they are not prepared.

Promoting an effective youth–adult partnership

Consider the following principles when deciding on an appropriate starting point for a youth–adult partnership:

- The parents, community and club must be clear that sustaining effective youth–adult partnerships can be a challenge for the youth service.
- The limitations of any responsibility given to young people must be clear and transparent.
- All partnerships hold high expectations of the people involved, and all responsibilities should be taken seriously with the people involved being answerable to others.
- Areas of responsibility delegated should be important and have significance consequence; otherwise, young people will feel inadequate in the partnership.
- Partners have to trust each other, but they don't have to be equal. Skills, money and confidence are often elements that are not equal in partnerships, so youth workers must keep this in mind. Trust, however, is fundamental to the success of a youth–adult partnership.

The youth worker's role in youth participation

- Have a clear code of practice outlining the policies and procedures in terms of health and safety and child protection requirements in the organisation.
- Commit to involving all young people in decision-making and forming a youth–adult partnership.
- Acknowledge and respect all the diverse aspects of young people's lives; their circumstances, backgrounds, interests, skills and needs are all different.
- Promote confidence among young people.
- Be realistic about the capabilities of young people; don't set standards too high too low, or have expectations that are not realistic.
- Provide opportunities for the young people to be involved in policy development and planning.

- Give freedom of choice.
- Encourage all young people to get involved actively by having an inclusive approach towards developing the youth–adult partnership.
- Meet the expectations of the club and the rest of the community.
- Motivate and support the group.
- Develop tools for checking that the partnership is working and everybody involved is getting something valuable from the experience, perhaps using a checklist drawn up together as an evaluation tool.

Youth–adult partnerships are invaluable to the participation process working well. To reinforce this practice the youth centre can draw up a Youth Participation Policy, which explains the organisation's attitude to young people participating in matters that affect them in the organisation. This policy, along with a Youth Participation Charter, should be drawn up together with the young people. A Youth Participation Charter is a document that helps to develop the youth–adult partnership because it highlights what the youth centre's beliefs and values are in terms of participation.

References, resources and further reading

Arnstein, Sherry R., 1969, 'A Ladder of Citizen Participation' in *Journal of the American Planning Association*, Vol. 35, No. 4, July 1969, pp. 216–224

Hart, R., 1992, *Children's Participation from Tokenism to Citizenship*, UNICEF, Florence: Innocenti Research Centre.

Shier, H., 2001, *Pathways to participation: openings, opportunities and obligations. Children & Society*, 15: 107–117. doi: 10.1002/chi.617. Accessed 25 June 2012.

'Why Don't We' is a Youth Participation Resource Pack available online at *www.youth.ie* which has a wealth of information for youth services.

Working with Groups

Stages of group development
Types of groups
Characteristics of an effective group
Different roles and norms
Group leadership
Theories of leadership
Leadership styles

Stages of group development

Group development is a seamless process that working groups are often not aware of but must go through in order to achieve the tasks set out by the group.

People play different roles in groups and they are usually defined early on in the life of the group. As the group develops, it goes through stages called forming, storming, norming, performing and adjourning.

Tuckman (1965) model

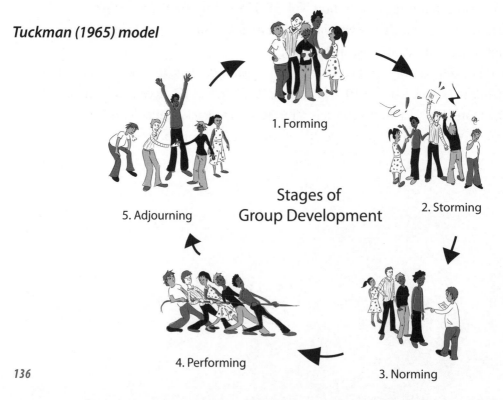

Stages of Group Development

1. Forming
2. Storming
3. Norming
4. Performing
5. Adjourning

The first stage is **forming**, when individuals come together with the same goal in mind. Most people behave well and time is spent on routines and the organisation of the team and conflict is usually avoided. People in the group are quietly forming their own opinions and some are making more impressions than others. This is a comfortable stage, but if the group stays at this stage the goal will not be achieved.

Storming is the second stage and the name suggests the meaning – people start to argue about how the goal is to be achieved, who has what role and where the responsibility lies. These minor confrontations will be dealt with or glossed over. While some people enjoy the storming stage, others would prefer to stay in the comfortable norming stage. It is important to move from this stage as quickly as possible regardless of conflict.

Stage three involves **norming**, which means that the group's tasks or responsibilities have become clear and agreed. Group behaviour starts to settle down and work is beginning to show results. The shape of the project is becoming apparent. Having had their arguments, the group now understands each other better, and can appreciate each other's skills and experience. Individuals listen to each other, appreciate and support each other, and are prepared to change preconceived views because they feel they are part of a cohesive, effective group.

The penultimate stage is **performing**, which indicates that the goal has been achieved and all is working well. Not all groups reach this stage. To reach this stage, it is imperative that the group moves through the storming stage. When performing is complete, the group is a working force. Individuals can work well together and can also be trusted by the group to work alone. There is a sense of motivation and loyalty within the group and it moves seamlessly to new goals and tasks. The identity of the group is well established, and energy and motivation are usually high.

Adjourning is the final stage of group development and is about the completion and detachment of the group, both from the tasks and the group members. Individuals will be proud of having achieved the goals they set out at the beginning, and maybe many more in between. Usually, group members are glad to have been part of a working group. They need to recognise and celebrate what they have achieved, and consciously move on.

Some authors describe stage 5 as 'Deforming and Mourning', recognising the sense of loss felt by group members from the group breaking apart.

Whether you are joining or managing a group, being aware of how the group is formed is invaluable; it makes you more aware of what is happening, particularly if the group and its task seem to be going nowhere. The process of achieving the task depends on the cohesiveness of the group.

Types of groups

There are a variety of groups that occur in youth work:

- Social
- Recreational or skill-building
- Educational
- Task/decision-making/focus
- Socialization

Table 3.3.1 Types of groups

Type of group	Description:
Social groups	Based on conversation. People like to get together just to talk; there are no goals attached; there is no leader.
Recreational or skill-building groups	People get together with a focus on a task for example football or scouts. The objective is to develop skills. There is a coach or instructor.
Educational groups	People join together to learn something new, for example a foreign language class or parenting classes. A professional delivers the programme.
Task/decision-making/focus groups	A task group is set up for a special purpose and is usually disbanded after the task is completed. This is called a task force. An example is a community clean-up project. A decision-making group is a sub-category of a task group that comes together to make basic decisions for the group, such as what resources they have and will need. This group could be used as a vehicle to working at local level. Focus groups come together usually before, during and after a project, and are used to identify needs, generate proposals and investigate results. They are used to acquire knowledge that can't be got from interviewing. There are formal leaders in all of these groups.
Socialization groups	Intended for young people to learn social skills such as making friends, conflict resolution, dealing with self-image, etc. The aim is to impart knowledge in a fun setting. There is a leader.

Characteristics of an effective group

- The group must have clear aims and objectives.
- The role of the facilitator or leader must be clear.
- Members should have good communication skills.
- All group members must be actively participating in discussion and activities related to the group.
- Group members should propose ideas and be listened to.
- Consensus must be reached before decisions are made.
- Once roles are identified for a task, members must be clear on their duties.
- Time must be given to evaluate the group's purpose, process and performance.
- Conflicts of interest are resolved through negotiations and mediation so that agreements are reached amicably.

Different roles and norms

By identifying the roles we play in a group, we can ensure that we use our strengths to the best advantage of the group and manage our weaknesses constructively. Raymond Meredith Belbin identified nine roles divided into three sub-roles. **Action-oriented roles** relate to the task at hand. **People-oriented roles** involve social interaction and **thought-oriented roles** are based on analysis.

Table 3.3.2: Belbin's team roles

Action-oriented roles	Shaper	Challenges the team to improve
	Implementer	Puts ideas into action
	Completer/Finisher	Ensures thorough, timely completion
People-oriented roles	Coordinator	Acts as a chairperson
	Team Worker	Encourages cooperation
	Resource Investigator	Explores outside opportunities
Thought-oriented roles	Plant	Presents new ideas and approaches
	Monitor/Evaluator	Analyses the options
	Specialist	Provides specialized skills

Throughout a typical youth work activity, such as an outing, these roles might be played out as follows: the action-oriented roles will be filled by the youth workers who get directly involved with the young people. The implementer will give out permission slips, collect money and book the bus. While on the outing, implementers will be actively involved in the groups' activities. The shaper will challenge the young people to try everything and get involved. The completer/finisher will ensure that everything runs smoothly.

The people-oriented roles will be filled by the resource investigator who thought of the idea, explored all the adventure centres and chose the best one. The coordinator will chair the meeting to propose the idea to the other youth workers and the young people. The team worker will provide support to all the youth workers and make sure the team is working effectively on the trip.

Finally, the thought-oriented roles are taken on by the person who thought outside the box, the plant, who might suggest that all youth workers who have children bring them along. The monitor/evaluator would analyse the pros and cons of what the plant suggests. Finally, a specialist might have the technical skills to put the photos up on the youth service website after the event.

 **Activity:**

Go to www.belbin.com and download the Belbin Self-Perception Inventory to find out what role you play in groups.

Group norms

Group norms are standards of behaviour that are acceptable to the group. As part of the establishment of a group, it is good practice to draw up a group contract. A group contract should include agreements on the following:

- boundaries
- respect
- trust
- listening
- confidentiality
- turn-taking
- punctuality

- discriminatory remarks
- aggressive behaviour

Group leadership

A leader is a person who supports and encourages a group of people to achieve attainable goals.

> ### Think about...
>
> ... leaders you know from work, school, sport or home. Think about the qualities that those leaders may have, and write them down.
>
> Examples might include: fair, firm, bossy, aggressive, being a good listener, etc. Such qualities may differ depending on the experiences you shared with the leader, and they may influence the type of leader you are or become. Leadership is a complex characteristic, and while there is no universal approach to defining or understanding it, considering some leadership theories and styles will give us a wider lens with which to examine it.

Theories of leadership

Trait theory

The Trait Theory is based on beliefs that leaders are 'born and not made'. Researchers believed that a person with this style of leadership was almost superhuman, with an exhaustive list of traits such as power, confidence, intelligence, aggression, imagination and loyalty.

Behavioural theory

Theorists soon accepted that it was impossible to measure traits like loyalty and confidence, but they could measure the behaviour of those who exhibited these traits; thus, trait theory led to behavioural theory. Research suggested that anyone could learn the traits needed to lead a group and have control.

Transformational theory

The transformational theory is based on the belief that people will follow a leader who is motivational and inspirational, someone who builds people's trust and develops relationships within the group. This type of leader is usually passionate about a vision and transforms people's thinking so that they too believe in that same vision.

Transactional theory

The assumption that people are motivated by reward or punishment is the basis of this theory. A leader would give clear direction as to what is required, and if a member of the group does not comply, they are punished. If they comply with directions given, they are rewarded. In this way, there is a transaction between the leader and each member of the group dependant on the member's behaviour.

Leadership styles

Broadly speaking, there are three main leadership styles:

Laissez-faire: The leader allows the group do as it pleases to a great extent. This style can work well in a small, well-established group with fairly clear objectives, but it does mean that the group can get out of hand very quickly.

Democratic: All group members have an opportunity to have their say before decisions are made. This works well as it allows individuals to feel ownership of a decision or a project and therefore they are more likely to be committed and stick with the tasks.

Autocratic or authoritarian: The leader makes the decisions and tells everyone in the group what to do. This is not to be confused with the leader taking responsibility in an emergency or crisis, as an autocratic leader will be the decision-taker at all times and for all activities.

There are advantages and disadvantages to each:

The laissez-faire style gives group members freedom and independence, but no one is taking responsibility for the group as a whole, so there may be a disregard for rules, a lack of direction or dissatisfaction.

The democratic style allows free expression, full participation and choice; it fosters equal rights; it is motivating and encourages involvement. The negative side can be that it takes time and energy to get things done, and some members may become bored with the lengthy discussion of ideas and arguments.

The autocratic style lends itself to discipline, security and everyone knowing what is going on, but it can foster resentment, fear, over-compliance, and a lack of trust and independence.

In truth, most youth workers use a combination of all three depending on the size and age of the group, their stage of development and their aims and objectives.

So, at the forming stage, the leader might be more autocratic in order to get things started. At the storming stage the leader might be more democratic in order to encourage commitment and involvement. When the group reaches the norming stage it may be possible to engage in a more laissez-faire style.

 Activity:

Think about the different types of group and different styles of leadership as outlined above. What style of leadership would be best suited to each of the types of group below?

Type of group	Laissez faire/democratic/ autocratic leadership
Social	
Recreational	
Educational	
Task/decision-making/focus	
Socialisation	

References, resources and further reading

Burns, J. M., 1978, *Leadership*, New York: Harper & Row.

Bass, B. M., 1985, *Leadership and Performance Beyond Expectation*, New York: Free Press.

Galton, F. and Eysenck, H. J., 1869, *Hereditary Genius*, London: Macmillan.

Hersey, P., Blanchard, K. H., & Johnson, D.E., 2001, *Management of Organizational Behavior: Leading Human Resources*, (8th ed.). Upper Saddle River, NJ: Prentice Hall.

Yukl, G., 2006, *Leadership in Organizations* (6th ed.), Upper Saddle River, NJ: Pearson Prentice Hall.

http://www.chimaeraconsulting.com/tuckman.htm [Accessed 7 June 2012]

http://www.personal.psu.edu/seh25/DeRueNahrgangWellmanHumphrey2011.pdf [Accessed 9 June 2012]

http://www.uc.edu/armyrotc/ms2text/MSL_201_L10a_Leadership_Traits_&_Behaviors.pdf [Accessed 9 June 2012]

Reflective Practice

What is reflective practice?

Reflective practice in youth work requires thinking about how you work and examining the experiences you have with young people every day. It also involves applying theory to practice. Reflective practice can be a challenging process, and sometimes it is done as a group effort when a youth work session is over. Reflective practice is a constructive and positive way for youth workers to develop an awareness of their strengths and weaknesses. Another benefit is that it constitutes continuous professional development. The reflective practitioner often takes on a dual role, analysing their own performance or behaviour and thinking about actions that affected their behaviour.

Boud et al. (1985) defined reflection as 'a generic term for those intellectual and affective activities in which individuals engage to explore their experiences in order to lead to a new understanding and appreciation' (p. 19).

It can be more beneficial for all if youth workers and young people reflect on the practice together, as this allows different opinions to be aired. It is however important to have procedures in place to minimise the possible negative effects of confrontations or personality clashes. Youth workers may also find it useful to take short notes after work to identify positive and negative things that happened.

People can find it difficult to reflect on what is happening in their everyday lives for many reasons. For one thing, we are all constantly distracted by external stimuli such as the demands of family, technology and pastimes. What's more, it's important to remember that our own behaviour is the hardest to analyse critically or to be objective about. For example, reviewing a recording (audio or visual) of ourselves can be surprisingly revealing.

Scenario:

Eric, aged 14 years, leaves school at 4 p.m. on Tuesday. He takes out his phone, sends a text, waits for the bus, checks sport results on his live sports results app, gets on the bus, and logs onto Facebook. He laughs out loud at his friends' comments and replies accordingly. He arrives home to have a meal and go on to PlayStation. After two hours of gaming, he decides he had better check Facebook again. He has received messages about whether he is attending the youth centre that night. He replies, gets changed and leaves the house. He spends one hour with his friends, goes home spends the rest of the evening on Facebook, his PlayStation and on the phone.

Consider the following:

- When did Eric think about his day at school, what went well and what didn't, and why?
- When did Eric talk to people?
- What will Eric do at school tomorrow if he is asked for homework?

There is only one corner of the universe you can be certain of improving and that's your own self.

– Aldous Huxley

In order to become a good reflective practitioner, it is important to be actively involved in reflection. Following a cyclical pattern is a practical way to analyse each area of reflection. This cycle consists of

1 questioning your work
2 thinking about the experiences you have
3 thinking about how improvements can be made

Equally important to this process is recognising successful experiences within the group and proactive methods of dealing with behaviour. It is hugely important to the personal growth and development of the youth worker that they periodically step back from the youth service to think about the positive things that have been achieved.

The Gibbs Model for Reflection (1988) is one of the most popular models for reflection, as it is one of the few reflective models that takes emotions into account. This six-step process encourages you to think systematically about the phases of a given experience. Use all the headings to structure your reflection.

The reflective cycle

Chart 3.4.1 Six stages of Gibbs' Reflective Cycle

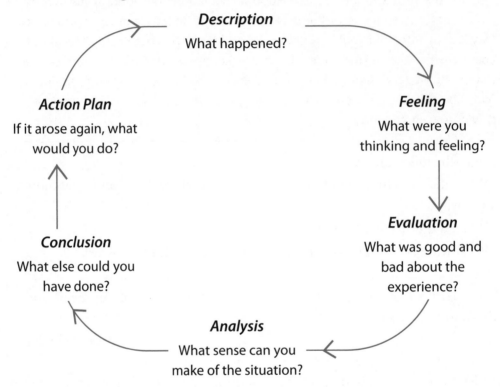

1 **Description**

    Describe as a matter of fact just what happened during your critical incident or chosen episode for reflection. Who was involved? Where did it happen?

2 **Feelings**

    What were you thinking and feeling at the time? And afterwards?

3 **Evaluation**

    List points or explain what was good and what was bad about the experience. Were things resolved?

4 **Analysis**

    What sense can you make out of the situation? What does it mean? What helped and what hindered it? Why did it happen? How did it happen?

5 **Conclusion**

What else could you have done? What should you perhaps not have done? What might you have done differently?

6 **Action Plan**

If this happened again, what would you do differently? How will you change your practice from what you have learned?

 Activity:

Paul, a youth worker, identified an incident that happened in the youth service where he works: one of the members arrived while under the influence of alcohol. Think about the role played by Paul, the young people and the other youth workers. Go through the six stages of Gibbs' Reflective Cycle, describing the reflective process that Paul went through.

Stages	Reflective process
Description	
Feelings	
Evaluation	
Analyses	
Conclusion	
Action Plan	

Use this template to analyse situations that you have come across in your workplace.

Types of reflection

Donald Schön (1987) and John Cowan (1998) identified and wrote extensively on different types of reflection, including:

- Reflection-on-action
- Reflection-in-action
- Reflection-for-action

Example:

Muireann comes to the Youth Centre every Monday evening. It is always a difficult time for Muireann because she stays with her Dad every weekend as her parents are divorced. She almost always causes a confrontation with others in the centre when she arrives. **Reflecting on action** (1), the youth worker is able to diffuse the situation rapidly because they know from experience that this happens most Mondays and they know how to manage it.

Reflection in action (2) occurs after the event, when the youth worker thinks about what happened and whether the action they took was successful or not. The youth worker may talk to fellow workers about the incident and Muireann's behaviour

Reflection for action (3) occurs when the youth worker and Muireann discuss this situation and devise a range of possible coping strategies for her. Youth workers must take time to think about a strategy that has the best chance of working. Doing so identifies a problem for Muireann and helps her cope with it; knowing that she has the support of the youth service helps her.

Identifying patterns and links in behaviour like the example above is the key to reflecting.

Reflective practitioners

Being reflective in your work

- demonstrates that you are actively concerned about and driven by the aims and outcomes of the work you are doing.
- enables you to examine, evaluate and improve your own work continuously, thus becoming a better practitioner.
- requires the ability to look carefully at how you work in order to develop new skills and an understanding of issues both familiar and unfamiliar.

To become a reflective practitioner you must:

- have an open mind.
- be open to learning and to changing your ways of work accordingly.
- be willing to enhance your own professional learning and personal fulfilment through cooperation and discussion with other practitioners.

Continuous Professional Development

Continuous Professional Development (CPD) refers to the continuing education and growth of a person as a professional. It leads to better work practices and happier, more fulfilled employees. Training courses, workshops, conferences, seminars, talks and launches of new publications and courses can all provide further knowledge in particular areas of interest. CPD improves staff moral and motivates people to work harder or to improve a skill they may feel they have lost. CPD usually involves people in the same or similar professions so that employees can make connections across their field easily; this kind of networking is invaluable for a professional.

What do youth workers achieve by being reflective?

- new and effective learning experiences for young people
- fresh ways of seeing familiar things
- personal and professional development in the youth work area
- continuous quality improvement of the service as recommended by the National Quality Standards Framework (NQSF) (Section 2, p. 6)
- a shared understanding of youth work amongst fellow youth workers

The role of the youth worker in terms of reflective practice

- to devise appropriate timeframes to allocate time for reflection, feedback to colleagues and for changes to be made
- to be clear about what requires reflection
- to be clear about who is involved in the process
- to be familiar with the theories of reflection and how they apply to youth work practice
- to be aware of how youth work is delivered in the service and to always strive for ways to improve the practice

To conclude, reflection is a skill that needs to be practised, but once it's mastered, the benefits for the youth worker both personally and professionally are invaluable in their career and in life.

References, resources and further reading

Boud, D., Keogh, R., and Walker, D., 1985, *Reflection: Turning experience into learning*, London: Kogan.

Gibbs, G., 1988, *Learning by Doing: A guide to teaching and learning methods*, Oxford: Further Education Unit, Oxford Polytechnic.

Schon, D.A., 1983, *The Reflective Practitioner: How Professionals Think in Action*, London: Temple Smith, 50–68.

Peer Education

What is peer education?

Peer education is the process of structuring informal learning among peers. This form of education should involve a two-way flow of information between peers. It is usually done over a period of time, focusing on a particular topic relevant to that peer group, such as safe sex or substance use and misuse.

A peer is a person of equal standing with another person in a group.

The most distinctive feature of peer education is that it empowers young people, because they are taking responsibility for their own learning. They can discuss topics openly and ask the questions they really want the answers to. Another key element of peer education is the youth worker's contribution. The youth worker must take the responsibility of ensuring that the mechanisms are in place to fully support and develop the skills and confidence that young people need to become effective peer educators. Mechanisms include provision of training, practical support and the removal of barriers.

Peer support, peer counselling and peer mentoring are three models of peer education.

- Peer support is popular in schools and is often referred to as the 'buddy' system, in which an older student will take responsibility for some aspects of a younger student. An example would be supporting someone through shared reading.

■ **Peer counselling** is one-to-one support for young people who are worried or under stress and provides someone of their own peer group for them to talk to about their problems. It can only occur if the young people are trained and know when additional support is required.

■ **Peer mentoring** involves motivating another person of equal age or status to reach their goals; for example, how to look for, apply for and find work.

The concept of peer education draws from behavioural theories such as the Social Learning Theory, Theory of Reasoned Action and Diffusion of Innovation Theory.

Theories of peer education

Social Learning/Social Cognitive Theory (Bandura, 1977)

Based on the work of psychologist Albert Bandura, this theory posits that people model all types of behaviour and other people are influenced by this behaviour. How much they are influenced depends on an individual's beliefs, values and how they interpret their experiences. For example, the famous footballers who model positive or negative behaviour have a powerful influence over young people. Whether it that influence effects a change in a young person's behaviour will depend on their own opinions, values and principles.

Theory of Reasoned Action (Ajzen & Fishbein, 1980)

This theory is based on the premise that people can consider the reasons for their behaviour and make choices accordingly. Thus, behavioural change is based on the person's attitude towards certain behaviour and what he/she believes will happen as a consequence of it, or as a result of what they believe other people might think of them as a result of their behaviour. Especially influential people, then, are those whom the young person considers to be important. For example, a young person is offered a cigarette; he does not like smoking and also worries about what his parents would think. The young person considers these things, which subsequently influences his behaviour; he rejects the offer of a cigarette. Another young person does not like cigarettes either, but is more concerned that his peers approve of his smoking than about his parents disapproval, so he decides to have a cigarette.

Diffusion of Innovation Theory (Rogers, 1962)

This theory is most often applied to how people can be persuaded to adopt the use of new technology or gadgets, but can also be applied to new behaviours in the realm of peer education, as young people are more likely to trust someone from within their peer group. A key element of this theory is the assumption that certain people (usually people we know and trust) within a particular population act as 'popular opinion leaders' (Rogers, p. 322). They spread information about and influence the adoption of an innovation or idea within the group or community. Therefore to be most effective, the peer educator must be a young person whom the others can believe and trust. An example might be a local reformed criminal who attends a service workshop to tell the group how it really is and what going to jail is like. In this instance, the peer educator has the experience, the reliability of information and the street cred to show the other young people that he has been there and is telling the truth.

To summarise these theories, people's behaviour can be influenced by role models and weighing up the pros and cons of their actions or following the advice of trusted friends and acquaintances can help us to understand why peer education can be a very powerful agent in bringing about changes in behaviour.

Role of the youth worker

The youth worker must first be trained to be a peer educator in their own learning environment before they can impart the knowledge, skills and training to the young people in the service. When a group of young people is interested in becoming peer educators then the youth worker's role becomes one of facilitating. It is important that everybody in the group be given the opportunity to avail of the training to become a peer educator. After training is completed, individuals should be free to decide if they want to participate in delivering educational programmes to their peers.

The role of the youth worker is to:

- facilitate the training of peer educators.
- build good relationships with the peer educators.
- promote the self-confidence of peer educators by trusting them to use their own skills with their peers.
- provide unobtrusive but consistent support.
- promote democratic development amongst the group.
- identify areas that need clarity.

- offer support where necessary.
- signpost where information and resources can be accessed for use in the programmes.
- allow time and space for the delivery of the programmes.

Guidelines for the youth service in facilitating peer education

1 There must be an overall coordinator to take responsibility for the peer education programme.
2 Participants in the peer education programme must be a minimum of 14 years old.
3 There must be a clear agreement or contract drawn up between the youth service and the young people that should contain:
   - a definition of the programme and the specific content being delivered (e.g. sexual health information).
   - the name and contact details of the coordinator.
   - details of the supports that will be offered by the youth service.
   - agreed ground rules which have been devised jointly by the group and the youth workers.
4 Access to information and appropriate resources should be available.
5 Support and supervision should be provided especially when young people are dealing with sensitive and controversial issues.
6 A review and evaluation process should be designed and set up for the peer educators and the youth workers.
7 Peer educators should be kept up to date with further training and conferences.

Characteristics of an effective peer educator

- being a team player
- commitment
- confidence
- self-respect
- communication skills
- respect for others
- openness
- motivation

Topics for peer education

Health and well-being issues include:

- ✔ Physical activity
- ✔ Diet and nutrition
- ✔ Sexual health
- ✔ Effects of legal and illegal substances on the body
- ✔ Mental health
- ✔ Emotional well-being
- ✔ Spiritual health

Social health issues include:

- ✔ Relationships
- ✔ Social status
- ✔ Gender
- ✔ Culture and subculture

General issues include:

- ✔ Economics
- ✔ Politics
- ✔ Legal issues
- ✔ Community concerns

Training methods for peer educators

Active and participatory methods of training should be used when delivering a peer education programme.

Table 3.6.1 Peer education training methods

Role Play	Re-enacting a scenario
Freeze Frame	The participants are asked to stop an activity or drama and describe how they are feeling at that particular moment as they freeze; they are also asked what will happen next.
Character Circle	One person sits in the middle of a circle and all the participants role-play that they are related to them, e.g. brother, aunt, granny. A telling getting-to-know-you exercise.
Brainstorming	Spontaneous generation of ideas.
Quizzes	Testing participants' knowledge before and after a session. Quizzes can also help to show participants that they may not know everything they think they know about a subject.
Games	Games can be used competitively or for applying theoretical knowledge to a practical skill.
DVDs	Invaluable visual aids for elaborating on a point, and a great way to break up intense theory sessions.

How to implement a peer education programme

Step one: Organise a focus group to help you choose your topic.

Step two: Devise questionnaires to find out exactly what the peer group wants to know about.

Step three: Research using the information from the questionnaire to focus your search. (See Section 5 for research methods.)

Step four: Liaise with specialists in the area in order to access accurate information on the chosen topic.

Step five: Decide on the training tools you will use such as PowerPoint presentations, video clips, pictures.

Step six: Implement the peer education programme.

Step seven: Evaluate the process.

References, resources and further reading

Ajzen, I. and Fishbein, M., 1980, *Understanding Attitudes and Predicting Human Behavior*, Englewood, NJ: Prentice Hall.

Bandura, A., 1989, 'Social cognitive theory' in Vasta, R. (ed.) *Annals of child development*, Greenwich, UK: JAI.

Fast Forward Positive Lifestyles Ltd., 2004, *Exploring the Depths: A resource manual for those wishing to develop peer education initiatives*, Dorset, UK: Russell House.

Murtagh, B., 'Peer Education, A Manual', Dublin: National Youth Federation and Health Promotion Unit.

Roe, B., 2001, *The Substance Use Peer Education Responses Manual: A resource for Developing Peer Led Approaches to Drug Education*, Dublin: National Youth Federation.

Rogers, E., 1962, *Diffusion of Innovations*, New York: The Free Press.

http://peoplelearn.homestead.com/BEduc/Chapter_4.pdf Accessed 20 June 2012

http://projects.exeter.ac.uk/europeeruk Accessed 25 June 2012

Good Practice Guidelines

Good practice guidelines: a Toolkit
Youth worker and young person
Programme provision and development
Policy and service development

Good practice guidelines: a Toolkit

Following good practice guidelines is a positive way to protect youth work values and principles in an ever-changing society that continually challenges young people and youth workers.

The City of Dublin Youth Service Board (CDYSB) toolkit provides excellent guidelines for good practice and it is recommended that the learner becomes familiar with this resource.

The toolkit takes as its starting point the following underlying principles:
- the young person is central to all youth work
- the health and well-being of the young person is of paramount importance
- the process is reflective and flexible
- all work involves thorough planning
- training, support and supervision are part and parcel of the programme.

The key areas are covered within three broad sections of the Toolkit, which are as follows.

Youth worker and young person

Building Relationships
Identifying the Potential Needs of Young People
One-to-one Planned Conversations
Group Work
Advocacy

This section suggests appropriate ways for the youth worker and the young person to form relationships, make plans, discuss goals, share skills and talents, explore interests, review advocacy and much more.

Programme provision and development

> Programmes
> Providing Information
> Activities Outside of the Youth Project/Service Premises
> Programme Resources
> Outreach Work
> Detached Work

This section includes recommended actions to provide planned activities, sufficient resources, opportunities for trips away, planned outreach and detached work.

Policy and service development

> Young People – Policy and Service Development
> Youth Workers – Policy and Service Development

This section proposes good practice guidelines for how both young people and youth workers should get involved in planning, devising and evaluating youth work policies. Areas such as the youth worker's role in policy development, compiling community profiles and continuous professional development (CPD) are all advised as good practice.

In the Toolkit under each heading there is a 'Statement of Good Practice', which is broken down into what the statement means in practical terms when working with young people.

Example: Statement of Good Practice: 'Activities outside of the immediate environment of the youth project/service premises involving young people are planned and organised with their co-operation and are undertaken in a safe and secure manner' (p. 26).

One of the many practical suggestions in the toolkit is that 'the youth project/service provide young people with an information card, to be carried at all times, containing essential information such as the organisation name, young person's name, accommodation details and youth worker's contact number' (p. 29).

It is important to note that some issues come up over and over again in different sections of the Toolkit, for example, issues surrounding child protection, health and safety, the importance of involving young people and the need for youth workers to work within their own levels of skill and expertise.

References, resources and further reading

Farrelly, J., Dunne, C. and Doyle, G., 2009, *Essential Guidelines for Good Youth Work Practice Toolkit.* Dublin: City of Dublin Youth Services Board (CDYSB).

Health and Safety

Safety, Health and Welfare at Work Act 2005
Employers' duties
Employees' duties

Safety, Health and Welfare at Work Act 2005

Every youth work centre should have health and safety procedures, which must be adhered to by all staff. Most often these policies and procedures for health and safety guidelines are set out based on the employers' and employees' obligations to comply with the Safety, Health and Welfare at Work Act 2005. The 2005 Act replaces the Safety, Health, and Welfare at Work Act 1989.

The Safety, Health and Welfare at Work Act 2005 sets out the main provisions for securing and improving the safety, health and welfare of people at work.

The Act sets out:

- the requirements for the control of safety and health at work.
- the management, organisation and the systems of work necessary to achieve those goals.
- the responsibilities and roles of employers, the self-employed, employees and others.
- the enforcement procedures needed to ensure that the goals are met.

Employers' duties

Employers (including self-employed persons) are primarily responsible for creating and maintaining a safe and healthy workplace. An employer's duties include:

- managing and conducting all work activities so as to ensure the safety, health and welfare of people at work (including the prevention of improper conduct or behaviour likely to put employees at risk* – for horseplay, see overleaf).
- designing, providing and maintaining a safe place of work that has safe access and egress, and uses a plant and equipment that is safe and without risk to health.

- prevention of risks from the use of any article or substance, or from exposure to physical agents, noise, vibration and ionising or other radiations.
- * 'Horseplay' and bullying at work would come within these categories.

Employees' duties

Employees (including full- or part-time, permanent or temporary employees, regardless of any employment or contractual arrangement they may have) also have duties under the Act.

They must:

- comply with relevant laws and protect their own safety and health, as well as the safety and health of anyone who may be affected by their acts or omissions at work.
- ensure that they are not under the influence of any intoxicant to the extent that they could be a danger to themselves or others while at work.
- cooperate with their employer with regard to safety, health and welfare at work.
- not engage in any improper conduct that could endanger their safety or health or that of anyone else.
- participate in safety and health training offered by their employer.
- make proper use of all machinery, tools, substances, etc., and of all personal protective equipment provided for use at work.
- report any defects in the place of work, equipment, etc., which might endanger safety and health.

To conclude, it is a huge responsibility to keep yourself and others safe and healthy in a working environment whether you are a manager or a youth worker. Remember to be vigilant in all aspects of safety, and remember that you are a role model for young people using the service, who will be watching your behaviour intently.

(Adapted from *www.mee.tcd.ie/safety/Act2005/shortguide_act2005.pdf*
Government Publications, Health and Safety at Work Act 2005,
Dublin: Stationery Office)

Child Protection

Please note: for the purposes of this topic, the term 'child' is used throughout (rather than adolescent or young person) to refer to all who are covered under the legislation – that is children from 0–18 years.

Increasing concern about child protection is rooted in profound changes in Irish society. In the past, the abuse and neglect of some children were often accepted as hard facts of life. More recently, the idea that children have a fundamental right to protection, whether there is obvious risk of abuse or not, has grown, and is now reflected in the legislation, particularly the Child Care Act 1991.

The Child Care Act 1991, which replaced the 1908 Children's Act, was the first piece of child-protection legislation enacted by the Irish State.
The Act has affirmed children's rights and needs and the concept of 'the best interests of the child'. The enshrinement in the Act of the principle that parental responsibilities are at least as important as parental rights points to a significant shift

in focus in terms of child protection. The child protection provisions of the Child Care Act 1991 were implemented by the end of 1995 but difficulties remain nearly 20 years later in relation to a scarcity of resources and how they are deployed.

Children First: The National Guidelines for the Protection and Welfare of Children 2011 (hereafter referred to as 'the National Guidelines') and *Our Duty to Care – The Principles of Good Practice for the Protection of Children and Young People* are the two documents laying down the principles and guidelines to best practice. The main elements of the legislation, signs and symptoms, the guidelines and principles will be given here, but in a book such as this, it is not possible to cover everything. It is essential that youth workers download or obtain hard copies of the two documents and read them carefully. Most organisations involved with children and young people today will offer some training in child protection and youth workers are encouraged to take up whatever opportunities are offered.

Historical perspective

In the past, children were considered to be the property of their parents, particularly the father, so parents could decide in what manner they would treat their children. Change began towards the end of the nineteenth century. In 1874, a scandal culminated in the setting up of the New York Society for the Prevention of Cruelty to Children. (The NSPCC in Britain and the ISPCC in Ireland are direct descendants.) Mary Ellen was an adopted child who was severely ill-treated, abused and neglected. Neighbours were concerned, but there was little that could be done because the parents 'owned' her; that is, until an enlightened lawyer decided to take a case against the parents under the laws relating to the ill-treatment of animals. He won the case.

In Ireland during the early part of the twentieth century, most child protection work was carried out by ISPCC officers, and most residential care facilities for children were run by religious orders.

While tragedies and enquiries pushed policy-makers into action, other influences were also at play. Civil and human rights were brought to people's attention across the US, the UK, Continental Europe and Ireland in the late 1960s and early 1970s. During the feminist movement, women took some of the darker issues from behind closed doors. Certainly, women's growing freedom to speak out about physical and sexual violence within marriage had a direct bearing on the exposure of child abuse in all its forms. Strengthening the rights of children generally has become a central issue in Ireland today that involves numerous groups and institutions. In February

2010, an all-party agreement was reached on the wording of an amendment to the Constitution to improve children's rights, and a referendum was held late in 2012.

The question of whether child abuse is more prevalent now than in the past is a difficult one to answer. Definitions of abuse have changed over time and there are variations in definitions between different countries, which in turn affects record-keeping and statistics and how they might be interpreted. If, for example, the present-day definition that beating children in school amounts to child abuse, then according to this definition it was rampant in Ireland prior to the outlawing of corporal punishment in schools in 1982. However, records of child abuse in schools would show that it hardly existed at all.

Additionally, there was little openness surrounding the whole topic of abuse, so that even those who were being abused according to the legal definitions of the time, had little chance of being heard or of having the courage to speak out.

Think about...

...levels of abuse. On a scale of 1 to 10, 1 being the least abusive and 10 being the most abusive, rate the following statements quickly: then reflect on the reasons for your choices.

  a. Leaving an eight- month-old strapped in the car while you go pay for your petrol.

  b. A father slaps his 13-year-old son who comes home two hours late from the youth club

  c. A mother always commenting negatively on their child's appearance.

  d. A mother feeding her four-month-old baby a tin of soup.

  e. An older sibling always physically and verbally threatening the younger one.

  f. A 14-year-old who hangs out with friends in an adult neighbour's house smoking dope.

  g. A 17-year-old babysitter drinking alcohol with friends while in charge of two toddlers.

  h. A 16-year-old working in an adult shop that sells pornographic material.

If possible, compare your ratings with another learner's and discuss reasons for differences if any.

(Adapted from HSE training material)

Some significant milestones in child abuse and protection since the enactment of The Child Care Act 1991

1992   **The X Case**: the State continues to protect the unborn child regardless of the circumstances of the girl or woman who has become pregnant as a result of rape or incest.

1993   **The Kilkenny Incest Case**: its subsequent investigation gave rise to significant improvements in child protection services.

1994   **The Kelly Fitzgerald Case** brought to light the shortcomings in communications between social work departments.

1993– 1996   **Madonna House, Goldenbridge Orphanage and Trudder House** were the first of a number of institutions where extensive child abuse, collusion and cover-ups were brought to light.

1994– present   **Catholic clergy abuse allegations**: cases of abuse of children by members of the Roman Catholic clergy and religious orders with yet more collusion and cover-ups.

1998   **McColgan v. North Western Health Board** set a precedent because a survivor of abuse successfully sued the Health Authority for neglect of its duty to protect her.

1998   **Protection for Persons Reporting Abuse Act**: under this legislation, no one will be penalised for making a report of child abuse in good faith.

1999   **Publication of *Children First: The National Guidelines for the Protection and Welfare of Children.***

2002   **Residential Institutions Redress Act**: the Redress Board was established under this legislation, and up to December 2005 they received 14,768 applications for compensation for abuse experienced.

2005   **The Ferns Report** dealing with the nature and handling of clerical child sexual abuse reports in the diocese of Ferns. Numerous recommendations were made which are currently being examined.

March 2006   **Dublin Archdiocese Commission of Investigation** was established to investigate the handling of reported clerical abuse in the diocese of Dublin.

June 2006   **Criminal Law (Sexual Offences) Act** rendered the charge of statutory rape no longer valid; the Act criminalises under-age consensual sex (under 17).

June 2006   Report of extensive abuse in a childcare establishment that caters for separated children seeking asylum.

Spring 2007	**Proposal to hold a children's rights referendum** to change the Constitution, with a view to strengthening those rights.
2007	**The establishment of Health Information and Quality Authority (HIQA)** within which the Social Services Inspectorate operates. The work of the Inspectorate has been focused on children in care, primarily on inspection of residential care.
2008	**The National Review of Compliance with** *Children First: The National Guidelines*. Many recommendations are made to improve the overall effectiveness of the Guidelines.
2009	**The Ryan Report**, the report of the Commission that investigated the abuse of children in institutions in Ireland. Many recommendations were made with regard to the safeguarding of children in the care of various institutions.
2009	**The Murphy Report**, a report on the investigation into the handling by Church and State authorities of allegations and suspicions of child abuse against clerics in the Catholic Archdiocese of Dublin.
2010	**The Roscommon Childcare Report**, a report primarily on the management of cases in which children suffered abuse and neglect of appalling proportions for years.
2010	**Child Death Review Group** convened following the unnatural death of two young people in care and the subsequent revelation that numerous other children had died. This group was set up to investigate the circumstances surrounding children who died in care or who had just left the care of the Social Services.
2011	**The Cloyne Report** on investigations, the handling of allegations and suspicions of abuse by Church and State authorities against clerics in the County Cork diocese of Cloyne.
2012	**Children First Bill introduced** which includes the proposal to place a statutory responsibility on all those involved with children services to report suspicions of child abuse (heretofore known as 'mandatory reporting').
2012	**Report of Child Death Review Group** established in 2010 (see above).
2012	**Launch of Child Rescue Alert Ireland (CRI Alert)** enables the Gardaí to alert and seek help from the public when a child has been abducted.
2012	**Referendum on Children's Rights**

Organisations and resources have now been established to deal with the whole area of abuse and to facilitate people who want to get help for themselves or for others. The National Guidelines set out clearly and in detail what action is required when abuse is suspected or uncovered. Childline was set up by the ISPCC with the specific purpose of providing a freephone service to children who wished to talk about their situations. The media, though sensationalist at times, has played a significant part in the dissemination of material in relation to child abuse.

There is no doubt that more cases of abuse are being reported and dealt with by the courts, and that more people who are being abused, or at risk of being abused, are receiving help. Child abuse statistics show that the number of cases which have been reported to the authorities increase annually.

Relevant legislation:

- Child Care Act 1991 is the principal piece of relevant legislation on which *Children First: The National Guidelines* is based.
- The Children Act 2001 (see Youth and Justice, p. 59)
- Domestic Violence Act 1996
- The Criminal Justice Act 2006 (see Youth and Justice, p. 59)
- Non-Fatal Offences Against the Person Act 1997
- Freedom of Information Act 1997 and 2003 give people the right of access and the right to correct the information that is held about them by a public body
- Data Protection Act 1988 and 2003
- Protection for Persons Reporting Child Abuse Act 1998 protects persons who report child protection concerns in good faith

*For further explanations of these and other enactments see Appendix 7 of the National Guidelines.

Definitions of child abuse

Different types of abuse are defined separately on p. 169, but in reality they are less easy to separate. When a child is being physically abused within a family, that child is also being emotionally abused. Likewise, a child who is experiencing sexual abuse is being emotionally and physically abused. The following definitions are those set out in *The National Guidelines 2011.*

- Physical abuse of a child is that which results in actual or potential physical harm from an interaction or lack of interaction on the part of the adult responsible for the care and control of the child. There may be single or repeated incidents.

- Emotional abuse is normally to be found in the relationship between a caregiver and a child rather than in a specific event or pattern of events. It occurs when a child's developmental needs for affection, approval, consistency and security are not met.

- Neglect is normally defined in terms of an omission, where a child suffers significant harm or impairment of development by being deprived of food, clothing, warmth, hygiene, intellectual stimulation, supervision and safety, attachment to and affection from adults, or medical care. Neglect generally comes to light in different ways over a period of time rather than at one specific point.

- Sexual abuse occurs when a child is used by another person for his or her sexual gratification or sexual arousal, or for that of others, e.g. masturbation or exposure in the presence of a child, inappropriate touching, intercourse, or sexual exploitation as in the taking of photographs for sexual gratification purposes. There is a wide spectrum of adult behaviour which constitutes sexual abuse apart from actual sexual contact, including non-contact activities such as obscene phone calls, offensive sexual remarks, voyeurism and use of child pornography.

Signs and indicators of abuse

Indicators of physical abuse

Explanations for injuries where the explanation is not consistent with the injury and/or frequency of injuries are cause for concern.

Physical signs

- Bruising in areas where bruises are not readily sustained, i.e. soft tissue areas (see Figure 3.8.1)
- Facial bruising
- Hand or finger marks/pressure bruises
- Bite marks

- Burns (especially cigarette), scalds
- Unexplained and frequent fractures
- Frequent and severe lacerations and abrasions
- Failure to thrive
- Poisonings
- Coma and death
- Fabricated illnesses or injuries
- Shaking violently

Figure 3.8.1 Areas of bruising

Normal: over bony areas   **Suspicious: over soft, fleshy areas**

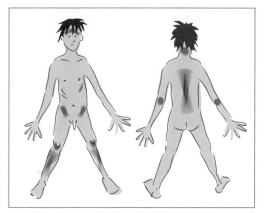 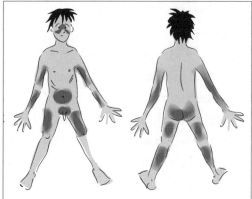

Behavioural signs

- Fearful and shying away from physical contact
- Frozen watchfulness
- Withdrawn or aggressive behaviour
- Sudden changes in behaviour

Indicators of emotional abuse

Emotional neglect and abuse can be identified with reference to the following:

- Rejection
- Lack of comfort and love
- Lack of attachment
- Lack of proper stimulation (fun and play)

- Lack of continuity of care
- Continuous lack of praise and encouragement
- Serious over-protectiveness
- Inappropriate punishments
- Family conflict and/or violence

Any of the above is more serious when clustered or consistent over time. It should also be remembered that any child who is neglected, physically or sexually abused is also being emotionally abused.

Behavioural signs
- Attention-seeking behaviour
- Withdrawn or aggressive behaviour
- Frequent lying
- Inability to have fun
- Low self-esteem
- Tantrums beyond the normal developmental age for same
- Speech disorders, particularly stammering
- Indiscriminately affectionate

Indicators of child neglect
Child neglect should be suspected when:
- There is abandonment or desertion.
- Children are persistently left alone.
- Children are left without adequate care and supervision.
- There is a lack of adequate food, warmth, clothing, hygiene.
- There is exposure to danger including moral danger.
- There is a lack of supervision appropriate to the child's age.
- There is a failure to educate or send to school.
- The child is failing to thrive.
- There is a lack of provision for child's medical and developmental needs.
- The child is exploited and overworked.

Physical signs

- Poor hygiene
- Inadequate, dirty, torn or inappropriate clothing
- Untreated medical problems
- Poor nourishment/emaciation
- Failure to thrive
- Being left at home alone

Behavioural signs

- Tiredness/listlessness
- Low self-esteem
- Inability to concentrate or be involved
- Constant hunger

Indicators of sexual abuse

Physical signs

- Bruises and scratches to genital area
- Soreness when walking, sitting, going to the toilet
- Pain or itching
- Sexually transmitted diseases
- Torn and stained underclothes
- Bedwetting, sleep disturbances
- Loss of appetite

Behavioural signs

- Hints of sexual activity through words, drawings or play
- Sexually precocious behaviour
- Use of sexually explicit language
- Preoccupation with sexual matters
- Informed knowledge of adult sexual behaviour
- Low self-esteem
- Withdrawn or isolated from other children

Particular behavioural signs and emotional problems suggestive of sexual abuse in older children (10 years +) include:

- Depression, isolation and anger
- Running away from home or care
- Substance misuse
- Self-harm and suicide attempts
- Missing school or dropping out
- Dropping out of activities
- Eating disorders
- Pregnancy

These lists of indicators, signs and symptoms for all types of abuse *are not exhaustive* and need careful assessment in relation to what is known about the child and family circumstances.

It is important not to jump to conclusions:

- a burn may be caused by a genuine accident;
- a sudden change in behaviour may occur because an elderly relative who requires a lot of care has moved in with the family;
- Mongolian blue spots, which resemble a series of bruises, appear naturally on the back and buttocks of some black babies;
- circular bruising may be the result of 'cupping', a Chinese medical treatment;
- masturbation and interest in sexual matters is part of normal development.

On the other hand, being aware of the signs and symptoms and always giving consideration to the possibility of abuse is important in the protection of all children.

Predisposing factors for abuse

Some factors (known as predictive indicators) have been found consistently in family characteristics and/or circumstances where abuse has occurred. However, the same factors can also be found in families where there is no abuse — *so predictive indicators of child abuse must be considered with extreme caution.* Statistics of child abuse show that child abuse occurs in all social classes, and the people most likely to abuse children are parents, partners of parents who are not the child's natural parent, relatives and neighbours, in that order.

Parental factors associated with child abuse

Parents who were abused themselves

A combination of factors are at work here, for example:

- Cultural: 'It didn't do me any harm, so it won't do my children any harm'.
- Past experience: Love and violence are confused because of the parent's own experiences of being abused by parents/carers.
- Poor role models for the parents: parents do not know other ways of disciplining and controlling their children because this is how their parents did it.
- Low self-esteem: parents may be emotionally damaged.
- Parents may be unable to control themselves.
- Parents may be unable to respond with warmth and affection.
- Parents may demand affection from their children in order to fulfil their own needs.

Very young parents

Emotionally immature parents may not be able to cope with the physical and emotional demands of a young child. There may be:

- conflict between their own needs and the needs of their child.
- a lack of support, or negative reactions from their own parents.
- an inability to recognise the needs of a child because of youth and inexperience.
- resentment of a child where there is a new and growing relationship between parents.
- The reality of caring for a child does not fit in with the 'dream' that is reinforced by society, e.g. that babies bring happiness, smiles and fulfilment, and that parents are never tired, frustrated or worn out with anxiety and worry.

Many youth workers may be involved with helping very young parents, so it is important to recognise the need for support and education in actual parenting.

Parents who expect too much of their children

- Approval and love are conditional on good behaviour and positive achievements.

- Skills and behaviour are expected of a child that are far beyond the child's age and stage of development, e.g. sitting quietly attentive for long periods of time.
- A child who fails to live up to expectations is seen by parents as bold, lazy or resistant. An example of this might be a baby who continues crying even when a parent has fed, changed, played with and cuddled them.

Parents who abuse substances

- Alcohol is often associated with violence; the adult may be predisposed to violent actions and reactions.
- Abuse of other substances may often be associated with neglect where money is spent on substances/drugs rather than on basic necessities such as food, clothing and heating.
- Abuse of substances may also lead to a general lack of responsiveness (inertia) on the part of the adult to the children and their needs.

Parents who are under stress

- For a parents who are overwhelmed by any problem such as debt, grief, trauma or fear, the demands of a child, even simple ones, may elicit an unreasonable response.
- Parents may blame the child partially or wholly for the stress.
- Parents may simply 'forget' to feed, clothe or show affection to the child such is the level of their stress.

The reason for a person's stress may not be obvious to an outsider. It is important to remember that what is extremely stressful for one person may only constitute a minor problem for another. **We must never judge the actions or reactions of another according to our own abilities to deal with stressful situations.**

Parents who suffer from mental health problems

- Mood swings and unpredictable and bizarre behaviour patterns can be very distressing and traumatic for children.
- Depression in a parent can lead to the neglect of children and an inability to respond to a child's needs.
- Post-natal depression can disrupt the bonding process and the mother's response to her baby in the early weeks and months.

It is now recognised that ongoing domestic violence in a family constitutes serious emotional abuse of the children of that family and the danger of actual physical violence increases over time.

Child factors associated with child abuse

Children aged 1–4 years

It is during this period that children demand the most attention. The novelty of a new baby has worn off, and a baby who has found its feet is much more demanding than one who has no option but to lie in the cot. At this period, the child is also beginning to assert their independence and individuality.

Children who are perceived as being 'difficult'

- Children for whom the early bonding and attachment process between mother and infant has been disrupted or weakened.
- Children who are difficult to feed.
- Children who are difficult to comfort.
- Children who are born prematurely, who may be a combination of all of the above.

Such situations may lead to overwhelming stress for the parent. Additionally, when children are difficult to feed or comfort, parents may feel a sense of failure.

Children who are 'different'

- A child who does not live up to the parents' expectations.
- A child who is not the sex that the parents wanted.
- A child who has a disability.

A child may be perceived by parents to be different without this being obvious to others; in these situations it is the perception that is significant rather than the reality. Basically, these are situations where the parent has rejected the child either wholly or in part.

The above factors may contribute to our understanding of child abuse and abusive situations, but many people lack resources and cope with highly stressful situations and/or extremely demanding children and would never resort to abuse. On the other hand, abuse can and does occur in families and to individuals who would seem on the surface to have no difficulties at all.

Especially vulnerable children

Part IV of the National Guidelines draws attention to children who may be especially vulnerable. These are children who:

1 *live in residential settings or are in the care of the State*, whether they are in foster care, care of relatives or in residential care. The establishment of the Health Information and Quality Authority (HIQA) and the Social Services Inspectorate (SSI), together with the development of national standards of care for children, should ensure the welfare and safety of children living in such situations. There are now also requirements for the development of child protection policies and procedures, staff vetting and training. Nevertheless, we can never become complacent or think that child abuse can never happen in such living situations.

2 *are homeless*, who are obviously particularly vulnerable, and the HSE has a statutory duty to provide accommodation suitable to each child's needs in line with the Youth Homeless Strategy 2001. It must be remembered that homelessness does not just mean young people who are sleeping rough (see Youth Homelessness, p. 247) but also those who are staying in hostels or in temporary arrangements such as staying with friends. A youth worker may be aware of such circumstances and has a duty to report the situation to the HSE.

3 *have disabilities*; research has shown that children with disabilities may be particularly vulnerable to abuse, and the abuser is most likely to be known to them. Children who have physical disabilities may be more vulnerable because of their needs for intimate physical care such as washing and toileting. Children who have learning disabilities may be more susceptible to suggestion or/and may not be able to express their difficulties and worries.

4 *are separated from their families and seeking asylum* and

5 *have been trafficked.* These children are more vulnerable for obvious reasons as well as for combinations of factors listed above. It is important not to make assumptions or presumptions in the cases of these children. Hundreds of separated children who are the responsibility of the HSE have gone missing in Ireland.

Peer abuse

Peer abuse is also given attention in Part IV of the National Guidelines and is of particular relevance to all those involved in youth work. The general guidelines are as follows.

- In a situation where one child is alleged or suspected to have abused another, the situation should be seen as a child care and protection issue for both children.
- The victim's welfare is paramount.
- A prompt response is essential, and concerns should be reported to HSE.
- Children who are abusive to others also require assessment, intervention and treatment. Early intervention has been shown to be most effective.
- Family support by HSE social work support is also crucial.
- Where abuse occurs in the context of a youth service, the impact on other service users and staff must also be considered and addressed.

The guidelines also cover sexual abuse by young people and note that research indicates that a considerable proportion of sexual abuse is perpetrated by young people. Four categories of behaviour are noted:

- Normal sexual exploration: if there is no evidence of coercion or domination, then this behaviour does not usually require child protection intervention.
- Abuse reactive behaviour: a child who has been/is being abused acts out the behaviour on another child. In this case, the needs of both children must be addressed.
- Sexually obsessive behaviour: a child is excessively curious or interested in sexual matters, or for example may masturbate at inappropriate times or places. The child's emotional and social needs must be considered and met.
- Abusive behaviour by adolescents and young people: here there are elements of domination, coercion, bribery and secrecy and must be taken seriously. An age gap between the young people or between the young person and child is an important consideration.
- Bullying: repeated aggression – verbal, psychological or physical – either directly or via technology by an individual or group against others. Having a policy and set of procedures in place is essential in order to combat bullying in youth services. Serious incidents of bullying should be referred to the HSE.
- Age of Consent: the age at which children can legally give their permission for their own participation in sexual activity is 17 years; therefore two 16-year-olds who are engaging in sexual activity are acting illegally, even though there may be no child protection concerns. If the proposed legislation in relation to

reporting such activity that is currently under discussion goes through, youth workers will be legally bound to do so.

Similarly, when a girl under the age of 17 becomes pregnant, a sensitive investigation to establish whether abuse as well as an illegal act has taken place is required; the HSE and the Gardaí should be involved.

Points to remember about child abuse

- The severity of a sign does not necessarily equate to the severity of the abuse.
- Neglect is as potentially fatal as physical abuse.
- Experiencing recurring low-level abuse may cause serious and long-term harm.
- Child abuse is not restricted to any socio-economic group, gender, religion or culture.
- Challenging behaviour by a child or young person should not render them liable to abuse.
- Exposure to domestic violence is detrimental to children's physical, emotional and psychological well-being.
- While the impact of neglect is most profound on young children, it also adversely affects adolescents.
- It is sometimes difficult to distinguish between indicators of child abuse and other adversities suffered by children and families.
- Neglectful families may be difficult to engage.
- Families where neglect and abuse are prevalent may go to considerable lengths to deceive professionals.

(The National Guidelines, 2011, p. 12)

Action when abuse is suspected

Figure 3.8.2 Child protection assessment and investigation process

Phase 1

I) Allegation or suspicion of child abuse.

II) Meeting with parents; it is essential that parents be informed about impending action unless that is considered to constitute additional danger to the child.

III) Referral to social work department by Designated Child Protection Officer (DCPO).

IV) Social Worker consults records and makes initial enquiries.

V) Social Worker consults with Team Leader/Senior Social Worker.

Phase 2

I) Notification to Childcare manager, options then may include:

    i) Notification to Gardaí

    ii) Strategy meeting with key people

    iii) Assessment of risk by social services team

Phase 3

I) Child Protection Case Conference

II) Negotiation of child protection plan involving all key people, including parents if appropriate

III) Treatment/intervention if required

IV) Child Protection Review

Before reading the following please study Figure 3.8.2.

The youth worker will be directly involved up to the decision to inform the HSE, and may be involved in discussions, case conferences or a court hearing if one takes place.

A student who is on placement should discuss concerns with their supervisor and their teacher. In order to maintain confidentiality, a student may seek guidance from a college teacher regarding the appropriate action to take, but they should not disclose the names of those involved. A student will probably not be involved beyond this.

Role of the youth worker when abuse is suspected

- Keep meticulous records at all times; these records must be dated and signed.
- Record only facts and direct observations; hearsay and hunches will not be admitted as evidence in a court of law.
- Discuss concerns with the DCPO.
- Interview the parents/guardians regarding their concerns about their child, unless there is reason to believe that this would place the child at further risk. The DCPO, supervisor or manager may do this with or without the member of staff who made the initial report. It is important for youth workers to be aware that the source of the allegation will be revealed to the parents/ guardians. If the case comes to court, the person who discovered the abuse will have to give evidence. It is almost impossible for the authorities to investigate, pursue and prove cases of abuse when those who gave initial evidence are not willing to be identified.
- Refer to the local childcare manager/social work team.

Allegations of abuse involving direct evidence or disclosure of abuse

If a child or someone else discloses facts of abuse to a youth worker:
- don't panic; remain calm
- reassure the person that they were right to report what they knew
- give the child time and opportunity to say what they have to say; they may not do this all at once
- avoid shocked or horrified responses
- explain to the child what action will be taken — keep it simple
- report the matter to the DCPO
- the DCPO should report the matter to the local social work team

Principles for best practice in child protection

- The welfare of the child is of paramount importance.
- A balance must be struck between protecting children and respecting the rights and the needs of parents/carers and families, but the child's welfare must come first.
- Children have a right to be taken seriously.
- Children should be consulted and involved in relation to all matters and decisions that affect them, taking into account their age and stage of development.
- Early intervention and support should be made available to children and families in order to minimise risk.
- Parents and carers have a right to respect and to be consulted about matters that affect their families.
- Actions taken to protect a child should not be intrusive and should minimise distress.
- Intervention should not deal with the child in isolation. The child has to be seen in a family context.
- The criminal dimension that may be involved must be acknowledged.
- Children should only be separated from their parents and family when all other possibilities have been exhausted.
- Reunion with families from whom children have been separated should always be considered.
- Effective prevention, detection and treatment of child abuse require a coordinated multidisciplinary approach.
- Any intervention should take account of diversity in families and lifestyles.
- Training for effective child protection should be mandatory in all establishments that offer a service for children.
- Roles and responsibilities should be clearly defined and understood within organisations and services for children.

(Adapted from The National Guidelines, 2011)

Remember:

- Leave verification and examinations to those who are professionally trained in the area.

  When physical injury or sexual abuse has occurred, the child will be subjected to at least one physical examination, whether you have already tried to look for evidence or not. It is good, professional practice to keep intrusion, questioning and stressful situations to a minimum.

- Do not offer false reassurance.

  'Everything will be all right now.' 'I will never let anyone hurt you again.' (These are examples of promises that nobody can ever guarantee.)

- Do not promise to keep secrets.

  In this way you will not have to break your promise in order to obtain help for a child in need. You can reassure them that you will not do anything without discussing it with them first.

- Avoid responses that lay blame.

  Do not question why the person did not act in a particular way, e.g. run away, shout, or tell sooner. Making suggestions as to how they could have acted is of little use after something has happened, and only serves to help the child feel that somehow they were to blame. Survivors are too ready to blame themselves as it is.

- Avoid telling the person how to feel.

  Horrified responses are often difficult to suppress, but strong reactions reveal what you think the child should have felt, i.e. 'Oh, how horrible', 'You must feel terrible', 'What a monster!' A child may feel confused, hurt, betrayed and indeed terrible, but you should allow them to express their own feelings rather than putting words into their mouth.

- Record what has been said as soon as possible, and in the child's exact words if you can.

- Your expertise lies in the area of being able to communicate with and comfort the child. You can provide an environment that will support the child at such a difficult time. You will be able to explain or interpret what is going on in a way that the child can understand because you will be familiar with their level of development, understanding and vocabulary.

Legal mechanisms for child protection

Emergency Care Order

This authorises the placement of a child in the care of the HSE in cases in which there is reasonable cause to believe that a child will suffer significant harm if not removed immediately from their place of residence.

An order may also be made if the child is likely to be removed from the present situation, thus placing him at risk, e.g. if a child is in hospital and might be at serious risk if returned home. The Gardaí, without a warrant, may remove a child to safety where they consider the child's health or welfare to be at risk.

Interim Order

This order keeps a child in the care of the HSE until an application for a Care Order has been processed and a decision made.

Supervision Order

This authorises the local HSE to have a child's health and welfare checked and observed, where there are reasonable grounds for believing that the child is at risk.

Care Order

This places a child under the care of the HSE. The HSE takes over the rights and the responsibilities of the parents and has legal responsibility to look after the health and welfare of the child.

The Child Protection Notification System

This is managed and maintained by the Childcare Manager. A child's name may be submitted for notification following a preliminary assessment where abuse is suspected or where it has actually happened. It should be constantly updated. There should be 24-hour access to the system; individual Health Executive Areas should have agreed on who may have access to the system and also set up procedures for identifying these people.

The Case Conference

The case conference brings together any professionals who have been involved and who have relevant information to share. It may include all or some of the above in addition to specialists, legal representatives and, increasingly, the family itself. The aim of the conference is to make decisions and draw up a Child Protection Plan.

The Guardian Ad Litem

The guardian *ad litem* is appointed by the court to look after the best interests of the child in difficult cases. The *guardian ad litem* does not necessarily have any relationship with the child but will read all files and case notes and provide an independent opinion for the judge as to what might best serve the interests of the child in the case.

Duties and roles in relation to child protection

Role of the youth worker

- To provide care and stimulation for each child according to each child's needs.
- To monitor the overall progress of each child.
- To maintain regular, accurate, impartial, dated and signed records of each child's progress.
- To maintain a close but professional relationship with parents/carers.
- To be aware of signs and symptoms of abuse in all its forms.
- To keep the best interests of the child in mind at all times.
- In times of doubt to be prepared to err on the side of caution.

Role of the manager/director of the youth work setting

- To ensure that professional standards are maintained.
- To ensure that records of all notes, logs and correspondence are dated, signed and maintained.
- To be aware of procedures to be followed in the case of suspected abuse.
- To liaise with the HSE and any other relevant personnel. If a report is being made the manager should use the Standard Reporting Form (see pp. 196–197).
- To provide support and in-service training for staff.
- To be prepared to take action in the case of suspected abuse.
- To provide direct support and counselling for any staff member involved in an ongoing case.

Role of the Designated Child Protection Officer (DCPO)

Designated Child Protection Officer is the title given to a person appointed within an organisation to deal with child protection issues that are brought to light. In a school, this could be one of the teachers. In a small scale service, it is usually the manager. Ongoing training for DCPOs is provided by the HSE and employing organisations. The DCPO's role is to:

- advise colleagues, managers and supervisors within workplaces about individual child protection cases as appropriate.
- advise on best practice and ensure that the organisation's child protection policy and procedures are followed.
- organise and/or facilitate child protection training and workshops for staff and volunteers.
- create and maintain links with the HSE and other relevant agencies and resource groups.
- report suspicions, concerns and allegations of child abuse to the HSE.
- facilitate follow-up actions.
- maintain proper records on all cases referred to them in a secure and confidential manner.
- keep up-to-date on current developments regarding provision, practice, legal obligations and policy.
- ensure that child protection policy and procedures are reviewed regularly and at least annually.
- ensure that the organisation's policy and procedures are brought to the attention of all employees and volunteers/students.

Role of the social worker

- investigate reports of child abuse.
- assess the risk involved and what action, if any, is required to be taken.
- keep relevant authorities informed of developments in the case.
- liaise with all relevant personnel, i.e. Gardaí, medical and referring personnel.
- maintain supportive and ongoing contact with parents.
- form a relationship with the child and maintain supportive contact.
- provide reports for case conferences and court hearings.

Role of the Gardaí

- investigate whether a crime has been committed.
- institute criminal proceedings against alleged abusers.
- provide back-up support for social workers, doctors, etc., if their investigations are being hampered or resisted.
- remove a child/children from immediate harm under Section 12 of the Act if the need arises.
- participate in strategy meetings, case conference and reviews.

Role of the Childcare Manager in the HSE

- take ultimate responsibility for the care and protection of all children in a given area.
- convene and chair the Child Protection Case Conference at which decisions about particular children are made.
- negotiate a Child Protection Plan involving all key people including parents/carers.
- ensure that decisions are followed through and that Child Protection Reviews take place.
- establish and maintain the Child Protection Notification System.

Supporting the youth worker

Youth workers, or indeed workers in any service, will be best served by adhering to principles of best practice relevant to that service:

- Every organisation must develop policy and procedures in line with the National Guidelines 2011.
- All volunteers and employees have a duty to care for and protect children.
- Safe recruitment practices should include checking references and Garda vetting. It is envisaged that the requirement to look for Garda clearance will be put on a statutory basis.
- Set clear criteria for membership.
- Records on all members and of all incidents should be kept.
- All buildings and facilities should be safe and secure and staff should be aware of who is on the premises at all times.

Adult supervision

- Young people should never be left unattended; supervision must be constant and adequate.
- Minimum adult:child ratio should be 1:8 with one extra adult; 8 or fewer children should be with two adults at all times.
- This ratio should change in line with ages, abilities and the nature of activities being arranged.
- There should be adults of both sexes supervising especially when the group is mixed.

Codes of behaviour:

- There should always be respect for a young person's space, privacy and safety.
- Workers should not give lifts in their cars alone with children.
- Where physical comfort/contact is appropriate, the worker must always be mindful of what is acceptable to and comfortable for the child.
- Physical punishment in any form is never acceptable and is against the law.
- Be sensitive to risks involved in some contact sports.
- Jokes of a sexual nature including those about sexual orientation are never acceptable.
- Over-emotional involvement between youth workers and children is not healthy for either party.
- There should be an anti-bullying policy.

Challenging behaviour:

- More than one adult should be present when challenging behaviour occurs.
- Record of the incident should be kept covering what happened, where, when, what was said, who was involved, details on any injuries and how the situation was resolved.
- Try to minimize drama that arises from challenging behaviour. The second adult supervisor can help to create distance between the challenging individual and the group if the individual cannot be persuaded to desist.
- What is and is not acceptable should be clear to staff and members so that boundaries and limits are clear. If staff members know what exactly they can do and what support is available they are less likely to respond unprofessionally to a situation.

When taking children away on trips:

- Pay attention to safety issues before the trip starts.
- Check that the organisation has insurance cover for all eventualities. Do not presume.
- Written parental consent must be obtained prior to departure and parents should have full information about all arrangements and activities including who to contact in an emergency.
- Records of medical concerns of any members including medication, allergies, phobias, etc. Details of any medicine being taken is essential in case of any medical problems or confusion, but also in case another child takes the medication for whatever reason.
- Sleeping arrangements should be worked out beforehand and members of the group should be clear about any rules and regulations.
- Maintain respect for privacy in dormitories, showers, toilets changing areas and so on.
- Employees and volunteers should not spend time alone with children.

Standards and good practice are harder to maintain when away as structures and timetables become more flexible. Experience suggests that more cases of alleged abuse are made during trips away.

Only about a third of cases reported result in court cases and care proceedings. For the most part, children who are at risk continue to attend their local schools and youth services. On the surface, it may seem that very few changes occur as a result of making a report, but the youth worker must continue to work with the child and family. If professionalism and impartiality are maintained at all times and the best interests of the child are always kept in mind, then it will be possible to re-establish working relationships with the parent, which may have suffered because of abuse allegations made by the youth worker. If all parents and young people are made aware of the child protection policy and procedures when they join the service, there will be more chance of maintaining a professional relationship in the event of abuse allegations.

For the person working directly with children and parents, the stress and anxiety incurred when abuse occurs cannot and should not be underestimated. If the youth worker does not take action, a child may suffer further abuse, and if the worker does take action, there must be adequate support from colleagues, management and other professionals.

Allegations of abuse against youth workers

When allegations of abuse are made it can be a very traumatic time for all those involved; the same is true when those allegations are made against youth workers. The procedures in place for dealing with allegations of abuse by any adult should also be adhered to in relation to allegations against staff. If the allegations are serious, then the worker will be suspended pending investigation.

In the case of an allegation against a staff member, there is even more need for support for the staff of the setting. The reasons for such support include the following:

- When abuse involves an outsider there are often one or two children involved; if abuse occurs within the youth work setting there may be several children involved.
- The staff member involved may be well known or a friend to other staff.
- Feelings of guilt or anger may run high among other staff members.

Poor professional practices such as shouting at children, ridiculing them, spending time alone with children or imposing extreme discipline should be dealt with through supervision, and a member of staff with poor professional practices should be helped with extra training and support to enable them to develop appropriate practices. Bad practice should never be condoned for any reason. This is especially pertinent in youth services with children whose behaviour may be very challenging.

Due to an increased awareness of child abuse, many people who work with young people – particularly men – are often fearful that they will be wrongly accused, and that it will damage them irreparably, even if the allegations are proven not to be true. If workers adhere strictly to principles of good practice then this is most unlikely to happen and the worker, if accused, will have the confidence that they have done nothing wrong.

Empowering the child

The encouragement and promotion of healthy social and emotional development is vital for the well-being of all children whatever their circumstances. Promoting confidence, independence and a sense of self-worth in children may help them to tell about some abusive situation or to avoid it altogether. Although it is essential that children learn some skills of self-protection, it is important to keep in mind that this in no way exonerates the adult from the responsibility of protecting them. Children cannot be expected to protect themselves and there is no conclusive research to show that children who have not been abused avoided it because they had any particular skills. Being skilled in any or all of the areas mentioned below does give children a greater feeling of control and perhaps assertiveness; research seems to indicate that in the area of sexual abuse it is often, although by no means always, the timid, unsure child who is targeted.

The ability of children to cope in different situations is greatly enhanced if they have been helped to:

- increase their self-awareness
- build up self-esteem
- develop the language skills to express themselves
- take control where it is age and stage appropriate
- cope with the unexpected
- identify their champions/people who will stand up for them
- develop problem-solving skills.

 Activity:

Aim: To identify ways in which the youth worker can help to empower children.
Plan a range of activities for children of different ages that would help them to master some of the skills listed above. The activities can be fun, but serious information can be given at the same time.

Example: start a discussion about safety. You are not supposed to leave the building once you have signed in until the session is over – but what if you discover a fire in a room at the end of the corridor?
Example: organise a role-play session that focuses on the difference between surprises and secrets.

When working with children, do not focus on abusive or dangerous situations since children will learn more easily from situations that are familiar to them.

Checklist

In the activities above, include some things that children need to know, such as how to:

- be safe
- protect their own bodies
- say 'no'
- get help
- tell
- be believed
- not keep secrets
- refuse touches which make them feel uncomfortable
- recognise when it is appropriate and sensible to break rules.

It is a mistake to assume that an older child or young adult will have learned these skills along the way. Many adult survivors' testimonies indicate that they did not know how to say 'no' or get help or protect themselves regardless of their age at the time.

Services for abused children

The main services provided fall into the following broad categories:

- prevention
- support
- investigation
- therapy

Prevention and support

The legal or statutory responsibility of supporting children and families at risk and of abuse prevention lies with the HSE.

Under the Child Care Act 1991, the HSE has a duty to:

- provide for children in need
- prevent ill-treatment and neglect
- promote the welfare of all children

Investigation

The legal or statutory duty to investigate cases of reported abuse lies with the social work team, the procedure for which has been outlined earlier in the chapter. In addition to the work of the social worker, other specialists in the area of psychology and paediatrics may be involved in establishing the nature and extent of abuse both physical and mental. Specialist units in the Dublin children's hospitals – Crumlin, Temple Street and Tallaght – deal with the investigation and treatment of child sexual abuse.

Therapy

Depending on the nature and the extent of the abuse there are many specialists who can help children and families to overcome the trauma of abuse. Social workers and psychologists will provide support and counselling. Qualified play therapists and occupational therapists may help children deal with their difficulties through activities. A psychiatrist may be involved if there are severe psychiatric difficulties. A family therapist may work with the whole family to help restore healthy family relationships. As indicated earlier, for the vast majority of children the best therapy will be to remain in the schools and services familiar to them and their family – indeed, in some areas there may not be any other options. When this happens, it is important that the youth worker liaise closely with any specialist therapist as requested. It is equally important that the worker recognise the effects of stress and trauma on children and be able to provide the appropriate support, care, attention, stimulation and environment.

Every child is an individual with a distinct personality, and therefore reactions to abuse will vary from child to child. Children may become aggressive and anti-social (fight) or become withdrawn, timid and sad (flight). Certainly, an abused child's sense of themselves as a worthy human being is damaged, as is their ability to form relationships.

Activity:

Aim: To become familiar with child support and protection services in your area. Services and facilities vary greatly from area to area. Consider the following:

- What are the child support and protection services provided by your local (a) HSE and (b) voluntary agencies?
- Do you have child protection policies and procedures in your place of work? Are they written?
- What is the name of the senior social worker responsible for child protection services in your area?

Abuse has meant that a child's trust in adults has been betrayed both by the adults who abused them as well as by all the adults around who failed to protect them. In general, children who are troubled are difficult rather than easy to work with; the anger of one child or the unresponsiveness of another may try the patience of the most dedicated of workers. Children who are severely damaged may need specialist therapeutic help but this will not be of great benefit unless the child also has contact with caring, consistent adults on a daily basis.

The overriding need of troubled children is for their self-image and self-respect to be restored. This may take a long time. It takes patience and understanding on the part of the worker to persistently and consistently endeavour to engage and support them.

Although the ultimate statutory responsibility lies with the HSE, voluntary agencies also play a big part in the area of child protection throughout Ireland. Barnardo's Child and Family Services and the ISPCC are the two main national organisations who work in the area of child support and protection.

Summary

The definition and understanding of child abuse and protection has changed over time. It is only since the 1970s that laws, procedures and policies for dealing with child abuse have been developed.

Research indicates that some factors predispose persons toward abuse, but these must be used with *extreme caution*; it is vital never to make assumptions or to jump to conclusions.

Good professional practice includes being aware of signs of abuse, drawing up policies and procedures and following these in all cases of suspected abuse whether allegations are against unknown adults, family members or staff.

All youth workers should be familiar with *Children First: The National Guidelines for the Protection and Welfare of Children 2011.*

The youth worker must be aware of the needs of all children and strive to empower them. When children have been abused, the worker must take their additional needs into account, especially their damaged self-esteem and the fact that their trust in adults has been betrayed.

Ultimate responsibility for child welfare, child protection and investigation lies with the HSE, but voluntary agencies also provide important services in the area. It is important to be familiar with the local services.

References, resources and further reading

Department of Children and Youth Affairs, 2011, *Children First: The National Guidelines for the Protection and Welfare of Children,* Dublin: Government Publications.

Department of Health and Children, 2002, *Our Duty to Care: The Principles of Good Practice for the Protection of Children and Young People,* Dublin: Government Publications.

Both of the above are also available on *www.dcya.gov.ie.*

National Youth Council of Ireland, 2012, *Protecting Children and Young People: An NYCI Toolkit for Youth Work Organisations to design, review and evaluate their child protection policies.* (Compiled by Olive Ring). Dublin: NYCI.

Barnardo's, 2011, *Child Protection Pack,* Dublin: Barnardo's.

Standard Report Form for reporting Child Protection and/or Welfare concerns to the HSE.

FORM NUMBER: CC01:01:00

STANDARD REPORT FORM
(For reporting CP&W Concerns to the HSE)

Feidhmeannacht na Seirbhíse Sláinte
Health Service Executive

A. To Principal Social Worker/Designate: _____

1. Date of Report [   ]

2. Details of Child

Name:		Male ☐	Female ☐
Address:		DOB	Age
		School	
Alias		Correspondence address (if different)	
Telephone		Telephone	

3. Details of Persons Reporting Concern(s)

Name:		Telephone No.	
Address:		Occupation	
		Relationship to client	

Reporter wishes to remain anonymous ☐   Reporter discussed with parents/guardians ☐

4. Parents Aware of Report

	Yes	No
Are the child's parents/carers aware that this concern is being reported to the HSE?	☐	☐

5. Details of Report

(Details of concern(s), allegation(s) or incident(s) dates, times, who was present, description of any observed injuries, parent's view(s), child's view(s) if known.)

FORM NUMBER: CC01:01:00

STANDARD REPORT FORM
(For reporting CP&W Concerns to the HSE)

Feidhmeannacht na Seirbhíse Sláinte
Health Service Executive

6. Relationships

Details of Mother		Details of Father	
Name:		Name:	
Address: (if different to child)		Address: (if different to child)	
Telephone No's:		Telephone No's:	

7. Household composition

Name	Relationship	DOB	Additional Information e.g. School/ Occupation/Other:

8. Name and Address of other personnel or agencies involved with this child

	Name	Address
Social Worker		
PHN		
GP		
Hospital		
School		
Gardaí		
Pre-School/Crèche/YG		
Other (specify):		

9. Details of person(s) allegedly causing concern in relation to the child

Relationship to child:		Age		Male ☐	Female ☐
Name:			Occupation		
Address:					

10. Details of person completing form

Name:		Occupation:	
Signed		Date:	

10.13.7.13 (12 Jul '12)

4

Youth Issues

Equality and Discrimination

Health and Well-being

Sexual Health

Substance Use and Misuse

Youth Homelessness

Information Technology and Social Media

The issues covered in this section are in one way or another relevant to all young people in Ireland today. The first part is designed to create awareness of individuality, equality and difference, in the first instance to examine the youth worker's own attitudes and bias, and then to consider the effects that prejudice and discrimination can have on the young people with whom they work. The following topics relate to aspects of health – physical, emotional, mental and sexual – that will enable the youth worker to consider how they can best work with and support all young people, but especially those who are negatively affected by some of the more challenging aspects of life such as addiction, self-harm, suicide and sexually transmitted diseases. Finally, any book on youth and youth work in modern Ireland could not ignore information technology and social media; the positive approach taken is one that will hopefully enable youth workers to take advantage of all that technology and social media can offer.

This section, then, is necessarily a bit disjointed in terms of the issues explored; the authors are aware that there are many other topics which could have been covered but hopefully the approaches taken here, along with the skills and knowledge learned, can be adapted and applied to other areas.

Equality and Discrimination

Self-exploratory activities

Each of us carries our own personal and cultural identity that shapes our attitudes to ourselves, to others and to the world around us. Youth workers need to explore and understand how attitudes are shaped in the first instance and how they can shape us. Therefore a series of self-exploratory activities are presented first, because any exploration of the area of equality and diversity must begin with oneself.

While most of the activities can be done by individuals, greater benefit will be gained in terms of knowledge and insight if the activities are done in a group setting, followed by group discussion. Furthermore, these activities can be adapted and used in a youth work setting. As best practice dictates, people should not be expected to reveal personal information unless they feel comfortable doing so. All participants must observe rules of confidentiality.

Activity 4.1 Individuality

Life may seem simpler when we classify and categorise; for example, when we label people as 'punk rockers', 'teenagers' or 'unemployed'. In doing this, however, the uniqueness of the individual is lost.

Aim: To explore and describe the uniqueness of the individual. The list below is far from comprehensive, but covers a variety of areas to show that our individuality is multifaceted. Using List 4.1, spend some time filling out details about yourself. Using what you've written, in a small group:
- identify what you have in common with one another
- identify what makes each person different and unique

List 4.1: Some details about yourself

First name
Family name
Colour of hair
Height
Birthday
Sex
Number of people in family

Place in family
Religion
Do you go to church/synagogue/mosque/temple?
Nationality
Hobbies/sport
Favourite band/singer
Favourite food
Favourite drink
Favourite film
What is your number one interest?
What is your number one concern about life/the world?

This list may be photocopied.

I am unique, just like everyone else!

A basic idea underpinning the concept of equality is the recognition of the dignity of individuals and their right to be respected as individual human beings. A genuine acceptance of this ideal means that individuals should be enabled to participate in society to the best of their ability; this in turn brings about some equalisation of power, wealth and resources. The acceptance and celebration of differences should lead to an overall balance and harmony among individuals in society. **This is not to say that people are all the same, or that they should be treated in the same way.** It is obvious that an adolescent is not the same as a child, or that a person who uses a wheelchair is not the same as a person who is walking. It is just as important to realise that one adolescent is not the same as another adolescent, or that one child is not the same as another child.

 Activity 4.2 Cultural influences

(This activity works best in a group context)

Aim: To raise awareness of diversity and to foster an appreciation of the complexity of identity and cultural/subcultural influences

From the List 4.1 on p. 202 select a number of the 'favourites'

- Food
- Drink
- Sport
- Hobby
- Band/singer
- Film

Use the completed list to introduce yourself to the group e.g. 'I'm John Murphy. I like pasta, and my favourite drink is ...' and so on. In the large group consider the similarities and differences between the group members. Identify as far as possible the country of origin of each item on the list, e.g. tea comes from India, potatoes originated from South America, pasta is associated with Italy. Sport may be difficult, but interesting! Use sticky notes to mark where everything originates from on a map of the world.

Activity 4.3 Celebrating diversity

Diversity exists even in a seemingly homogenous group. (Homogenous means all the same or similar, for example all 12-year-old girls). Within any particular group, regardless of how much they may have in common, people will have different backgrounds, talents, likes and dislikes – just think of a group of 12-year-old girls!

Look at the answers you have written on List 4.1. Share with the whole group:

- one thing that you think you have in common with the group.
- one thing that you think makes you different from the rest of the group.

List the differences and the similarities on a chart.

Activity 4.4: Values and roles

Aim: This activity explores how roles are filled in families and if there are any identifiable patterns.

The beliefs and values that shape our behaviour come from our parents, families, friends, peer group, community and the society in which we live. The family has a primary influence on what we learn about social roles and behaviour, both our own and those of others.

Read the tasks in List 4.2 and place in their order of importance a) for you personally and b) the order of importance that you believe society places on them. Think about and discuss why some tasks are more valued than others.

List 4.2 Household tasks

Cooking
Cleaning
Food shopping
Mowing the lawn
Weeding the garden
Household repairs
Paying bills
Filling the dishwasher
Tidying up
Looking after the car
Looking after people when they are ill

This list may be photocopied.

Extensions to these activities:

Discuss how a youth worker might adapt these exercises to enable young people to explore issues of identity and values and to celebrate diversity in the youth service and in their community. The lists may be photocopied and/or amended or extended to make the exercise more relevant to different groups.

Reflect in writing what you have learned from any of these exercises; include in a Reflective Journal.

Definitions

The following will introduce and explore some of the main terms and concepts associated with equality and diversity.

- **Equality** is about ensuring that people are being afforded equal rights and opportunities regardless of any differences they may have.
- **Diversity** is achieved when a group or society is made up of a range of many people who are different from each other, such as a mix of people who are old, young, men, women, black, white, blind, arty, sporty, etc.
- **Stereotype** is defined as a simplistic generalisation about or caricature of any individual or group. A stereotype is often derogatory, i.e. a put-down. It attributes characteristics to individuals on the basis of the group to which they are seen to belong and makes no allowance for individual differences.
- **Prejudice** is defined as an attitude, judgement or feeling formed without any direct knowledge of the group or individual but based on preconceived ideas or stereotypes. Prejudice can be positive as well as negative and *we all have some prejudices.*
- **Anti-bias** or **anti-prejudice** refers to programmes or activities that actively seek to develop a mental attitude of openness and acceptance by dispelling ignorance and spreading knowledge.
- **Labelling** identifies an individual or group by reference to one characteristic or perceived characteristic of that person or group; the term 'classifying' can also be used.
- **Scapegoating** occurs when an individual or group wrongly blames another individual or group against whom they are prejudiced. For example, young people are often blamed for monopolising health and hospital services by binge drinking and taking drugs, when in reality older people who

drink heavily are much more likely to have both chronic and acute health problems.

■ **Stigma** refers to a name or stereotype to which shame, disgrace or negative connotations are attached. Some acceptable terms in common use are stigmatising because they highlight an undesirable characteristic and devalue the individual, e.g. poor, mentally ill, criminal, handicapped, etc. Even 'teenager' is sometimes be used negatively for example in the media.

■ **Discrimination** is the result of policies, practices or behaviour that leads to the unfair treatment of individuals or groups because of their identity or perceived identity. *Prejudice translated into action becomes discrimination.* There are three main forms of discrimination: these are as outlined in the legislation. For more detail on the legislation see Equality and the law, p. 217.

■ **Direct discrimination:** treating someone unfairly solely because of their perceived difference, e.g. because they are young: 'Only two young people are allowed to enter this shop at anyone time.'

■ **Indirect discrimination:** setting down conditions that automatically disqualify certain people *without*

good reason, e.g. job advertisements that specify 'Applicants must have fluent English.' 'Applicants must be over 25.'

■ **Discrimination by association** happens when a person is treated less favourably because of their association with someone else.

■ **Unequal burdens:** failing to remove obstacles that exclude certain people, e.g. lack of ramps or lifts in a building automatically disbars people who use wheelchairs.

 Activity 4.5: Understanding definitions

For each of the following statements, identify which is an example of the terms explained above. Make up some more statements to help you apply the terms in practice.

- 'You couldn't trust a woman to run a large business because she wouldn't be able to keep her head in a crisis.'
- 'All young lads are thugs.'
- 'Boys are naturally better at sports than girls.'
- 'Asthmatics must be careful to avoid undue stress.'
- 'Room 3a is where the special needs kids go for extra classes.'
- 'Girls are obsessed with weight and body image.'
- 'Children must not play on the grass.'
- 'Teenagers are irresponsible.'

Activity 4.6: Discrimination

We all have prejudices to some degree – it is part of human nature. Being aware of our attitudes and prejudices and how they can affect us and others is an important step in developing a more just and equal society.

Write about two instances of discrimination which you have personally experienced. What happened? How did you feel?

Write about two instances when you have shown prejudice or discrimination toward another. What happened? How did you feel?

These can be related to age, gender, education or any other issue.

If working in a group, people can share their experiences in discussion or what has been written can be pinned to a board anonymously or read out by the group leader or youth worker and discussion can be based around these.

Power is essential to discrimination. No other person can discriminate against you, or in your favour, unless that person has the power to do so. Think of the individuals and groups who have power in our society and those who lack power: it is not politicians, bankers or bishops who suffer from prejudice or discrimination; it is the poor, Travellers, people who have a disability and indeed young people who lack power.

Activity 4.6: Language matters

Divide into groups of three or four. Give each group a copy of the 'Language Matters' worksheet.

In the groups, discuss the names we use to describe people, using these questions:

- Which names are in common use?
- Which names might the people being described prefer to be called?
- Why do people use different versions of names?

Ask the group to add some more and also fill in the empty spaces with different examples.

- Which names are positive and which are negative?

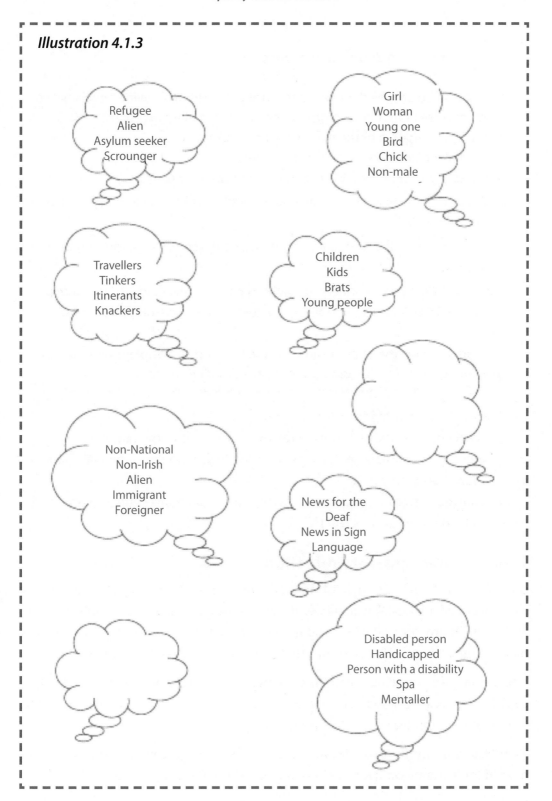

Illustration 4.1.3

Activity 4.7: Unequal chances

This activity can only be done by a large group. The group is divided into smaller groups of three or four in each group. The task is to make a greeting card for any occasion: Valentine's, a birthday, congratulations, etc.

Materials are divided unequally as follows:
- Group 1 gets a sheet of A4 white paper and two lead pencils.
- Group 2 gets a sheet of A4 white paper, a lead pencil, four coloured pencils and a piece of string.
- Group 3 gets 2 sheets of coloured paper, coloured markers, glitter glue and scissors.
- Group 4 gets several sheets of coloured paper, some coloured tissue paper, coloured markers including silver and gold, stickers, scissors and stamps.

…and so on. When the cards are finished, pin them up on a display board and ask a person from outside the group to come in and 'judge' the cards.

Ask the groups and individuals to:
a) reflect on how they felt during the exercise and after the judging;
b) identify individuals and groups of individuals who have unequal chances in Irish society today;
c) consider the consequences of having unequal chances; how might such individuals or groups react?

Young people and discrimination

The National Youth Council of Ireland together with the Equality Authority commissioned a study, 'Inequality and the Stereotyping of Young People' (Devlin, 2006), which provides valuable insights and information into the topic. The themes that emerged from the focus groups that formed the basis of the study were:

The media has a powerful role in the depiction of young people, and most often that depiction is negative; good news about young people is limited and often only to be found in programmes or articles aimed at children.

The local community provides few facilities for young people, so they often get hassled for 'hanging out'; seen as 'looking for trouble' and 'up to no good'.

The Gardaí in general have a poor view of young people, especially when groups were involved; not being taken seriously by the Gardaí was another concern.

Going shopping was a particular area where young people felt that adults clearly did not trust them, especially if they were in groups.

Politicians' attitudes towards young people was generally believed to be negative, although that worked both ways. Politicians were seen by young people as being old and young people viewed themselves as voiceless.

Teachers and school – though the attitude depended very much on individual teachers, there was a consensus that young people had little say in decision-making in their schools, and a feeling that some rules and arrangements were simply unfair.

Relationships between adults and young people and respect – adults in general hold stereotypical views of young people and as a result relationships between them tended to be unequal and sometimes unfair.

The study also looks at the portrayal of young people in the press and reports findings from other countries. Taken all together, the conclusion was that young people are indeed stereotyped in the media and viewed negatively by adults in general (although individual adults may have positive views). These facts affect young people's ability to have their voices heard, and also affect how they in turn view the adult world or the area in which they live.

Another interesting fact that emerges from the study is that young people from marginalised groups experience stereotyping and discrimination at even more complex levels. Young people with disabilities were treated differently than other young people based on their disability because those in authority often expected less of them, and they often found it difficult to get involved in local youth culture because of segregated education. Those from disadvantaged areas experience more extreme stereotyping and negative reactions from adults and institutions; those who had immigrated to Ireland experience stereotyping related to their 'foreignness'. Young men had often experienced more negative attitudes and reactions than did young women. So not all experiences are the same, but the study does seem to suggest that there is a definite trend in the stereotyping of the young.

Activity 4.8: Young people in the media

Investigate how young people are portrayed in the media by:
a) looking at media images
b) examining the language used
c) identifying the underlying views and assumptions

Evidence
Collect newspaper and magazine articles over a period of time; look at news and current affairs for a specified period. Carry out a content analysis using the following guidelines:

Media image
What is the first thing you think when you look at the image?
Is it a positive or negative image? Why?
Is there a stereotype suggested by the image?

Language used
Is the title positively or negatively worded?
What actual word is used to convey the age of the people involved?
What is the theme of the article/programme?

Opinion
Why is the piece newsworthy?
Whose opinion is given?
How would you feel if this article were about you or a member of your family?

Marginalised young people

Lalor et al (2007) examined the situation of some marginalised young people in Ireland and highlighted some alarming aspects of the effects of prejudice and discrimination in our society.

Young people with disabilities
- Diminished participation in education.
- Less is expected of them by teachers, leading to low achievement.
- Leave school with fewer qualifications.

- Higher levels of unemployment.
- Fewer options for leisure activities.
- More difficult to express their sexuality.
- Poor access to services that are not 'specialised'.
- Often experience pitying and patronising behaviour from others.

Young Travellers

- Accommodation and living conditions in general are inferior and there is less choice of location.
- Only a minority of Travellers complete secondary education and only a handful go on the third level.
- Levels of literacy are much lower.
- Levels of employment are much lower than those of young people in the settled community.
- Participation in sport and other leisure activities is less common or segregated.
- Frequent discrimination.
- Incidence of ill health, both mentally and physically, is higher.

One-third of the Traveller population is under 25 years of age, so the community has a higher proportion of young people.

Young people from immigrant populations

- Difficulty participating fully in education.
- If in Direct Provision Accommodation they receive €19.60 per week in contrast to €100 to which eligible young Irish people may be entitled.
- Accommodation for immigrant young people and unaccompanied minors are not subject to the same inspection arrangements as those for Irish young homeless people.
- Unaccompanied minors appear to have less social care and less social work support.
- Culture-based behaviour may be misunderstood or cause conflicts, e.g. dress code or difficulties with the Irish drinking culture.
- Misunderstanding in terms of beliefs, values and even what is meant by youth itself. As mentioned in the section on adolescence, norms and customs or the

concept of adolescence itself may be strange to young people from another culture.

- Protection and rescue may not be readily accessible to young people who are being exploited or trafficked.
- Frequent verbal abuse, name-calling and physical attacks due to racism and xenophobia.

Young people in care or leaving care

- Greater difficulties with employment, accommodation, addiction, prostitution and crime.
- Consistent and dependable adult support is often lacking.
- Fewer go on to third level education.
- There is a stigma attached to having been in care.

Young homeless people

- Education tends to be disrupted or cut short.
- Access to support and health services is curtailed.
- Employment is virtually impossible.
- Dependent on outreach services.
- Open to exploitation and victimisation both physical and sexual.
- Vulnerable to substance misuse.
- Experience lack of security.
- The stigma of homelessness is powerful, with blame falling on the young people themselves.

Young people from rural areas

- Less access to services and less variety of services.
- Lack of transport.
- A smaller population of other young people with whom to share their interests.
- May be removed from youth culture, although technology and social media may have positive effect here.
- Employment may be much more difficult to find.
- Young men and women may be more bound by conservative gender role expectations.

- People who are in the other marginalised groups above are likely to be even more isolated and marginalised in rural areas.

Equality and the law

Martin Luther King, Jr., the US civil rights leader of the 1960s, reflected on the fact that laws cannot change what is in a person's heart, but they can change what that person is able to do about what is in their heart. The law is there to protect people. It also serves a purpose in demonstrating society's opposition to intolerance and discrimination: it should also promote positive action. The enforcement of laws may help to bring about some changes in attitudes as enforcement demonstrates a commitment to the values and concepts underpinning the laws.

The basic principle underlying equality legislation today is that people should, in general, be judged on their merits as individuals rather than by reference to irrelevant characteristics over which they have no control. Currently the two principal pieces of legislation are The Employment Equality Acts 1998 and 2004, and The Equal Status Acts 2000 to 2004.

Both pieces of legislation prohibit discrimination on the following nine grounds:

1 Gender
2 Marital status
3 Family status
4 Sexual orientation
5 Religious belief
6 Age
7 Disability
8 Race
9 Membership of the Traveller Community

■ Gender – Gender and sex are now often used interchangeably, but there are important differences relevant to equality and diversity in the meaning of the two words. Sex refers to biological differences, which are used to distinguish males from females. Gender relates to society's ideas about appropriate masculine and feminine roles and characteristics. While the biological differences between men and women are the same the world over, gender differences may vary from society to society and in different eras. *Sexism* means prejudice or discrimination in relation to a person's gender.

- Marital status – whether a person is single, married, separated, divorced or widowed.
- Family status – whether a person or their partner is pregnant, has or does not have children under 18, or is the resident primary carer of a person with a disability of any age.
- Religion – one's religious belief, affiliation or lack thereof.
- Age – Relevant in terms of discrimination only to a person over 18 years, except for the provision of car insurance. The Childcare Act 1991 is the relevant legislation in relation to persons under 18 years.

    Prejudice or discrimination in relation to a person's age is called *ageism.*
- Sexual orientation – Refers to whether a person is attracted to men, women or both in their choice of sexual partner.

Employment Equality Acts 1998 and 2004

- prohibit discrimination by employers, collectives, advertising, employment agencies, vocational training authorities and by vocational bodies (i.e. professional associations and trade unions) in advertisements and in recruitment.
- define sexual harassment for the first time in Irish law.
- support positive action regarding age, disability, gender and Travellers.
- established a statutory office of Director of Equality Investigations.

Equal Status Acts 2000 and 2004

- prohibit discrimination in relation to the provision of goods and services, the obtaining and disposal of accommodation, and access to and participation in education. All services that are generally available to the public are covered, whether statutory or private.
- prohibit sexual harassment or victimisation.
- require reasonable accommodation of people with disabilities.
- allow for positive action to promote equality of opportunity and to cater for people who have additional needs.

The weakness of the legislation is that it does not clearly and unequivocally state rights for minority groups, nor does it recognise that discrimination on the grounds of social class is widespread. Sufficient resources have not been allocated to ensure the effective enforcement of the legislation.

The Equality Authority

The Equality Authority is an independent body with five main functions:
1 To combat discrimination in the areas covered by the Acts.
2 To promote equality of opportunity in matters to which the legislation applies.
3 To provide information to the public through a range of formats and media.
4 To monitor and review the operations of the Acts outlined above.
5 To make recommendations to the Minister for Justice, Equality and Law Reform as appropriate.

The Equality Authority has an in-house legal service that may, at its discretion, provide a free, confidential advisory service.

The Equality Tribunal

The purpose of the Equality Tribunal is to investigate, mediate and decide in claims of unlawful discrimination. Where it has been established that there has, in fact, been discrimination, an equality officer may order one or more of the following: compensation, equal pay, arrears of wages, equal treatment, or a specified course of action. Such orders are legally binding.

The UN Convention on the Rights of the Child 1989 sets out the right of all children to grow up in an environment that is free from prejudice and discrimination and one which enhances each child's self-image. The principle of equality pervades the Universal Declaration of Human Rights. It is in the valuing of differences and diversity that we embrace the real principles of fairness and justice for all regardless of gender, class, race, religion, age, marital status, ethnic group, ability and sexual orientation. It is essential to explore how an environment committed to equality promotes an all-round positive attitude to oneself and others. The role of the youth worker is explored as it is central to the existence of such an environment.

Role of the youth worker

To empower young people means to:

- develop their confidence, autonomy, independence and competence.
- develop their skills and strategies for coping with discriminatory behaviour.
- enable young people to develop their awareness and understanding.
- question false and unfair assumptions about the world and people around them.
- challenge damaging attitudes and practices.

Youth workers should ensure that young people feel:

- **valued** by knowing their names, their likes and dislikes, listen to them, show them respect.
- **liked** by giving them time, showing appropriate affection, smiling and generally showing that youth workers like being with them.
- **secure** by accepting them, providing consistently clear and fair boundaries, and giving them some privacy.
- **supported** by letting them know that nobody is allowed to put down, tease or exclude them on the basis of a perceived difference such as size, hair colour, skin colour, gender, sexual orientation, ability and so on.
- **that their family type is accepted** by inclusion in the resources of the setting with representations in books and posters of all types of families — large, small, one-parent, blended and extended.
- **that their ideas and skills are valued** by offering to display all work and giving all participants an opportunity to help regularly with different tasks suited to their ability and talents.
- **that assumptions are not made about them** by not discriminating against them; boys as well as girls like to be complimented on their appearance; both are equally good at cleaning and tidying if they get guidance and support; girls as well as 'big strong boys' can help with fetching and carrying. A young person whose income (or that of the family) is from social welfare may be hurt if not asked to bring in the same as everyone else, even though the youth worker may have felt that it would put too much pressure on the young person or their parents. A young person may, or may not, want to participate in Christmas or Easter if they are not Christian.

- **that their emotions are acknowledged.** Encourage young people to recognise, acknowledge and express their feelings in an acceptable manner. Acknowledge your own feelings, and be a positive role model on how feelings can be dealt with.
- **that they are allowed to take some control in their lives.** All young people should have a voice, an opportunity to speak and to make choices, and be involved in decisions that affect them.

Responding to the individuality of each person is the cornerstone principle in the provision of an environment committed to equality and anti-bias practice. This approach supports and affirms the young person, their family, home background and community. It stretches the experiences of young people to take account of the diversity that exists in their group, community and country.

An environment committed to equality aims to:

- **free young people from limiting stereotypical definitions** which may close off aspects of their development.
- **promote the self-esteem of individuals** by enabling them to feel positive about themselves. Effort should be appreciated rather than results rewarded.
- **promote and value individual development** by facilitating each one's participation in activities necessary for physical, cognitive, social and emotional growth.
- **develop each young person's skill in questioning and challenging stereotypes.** Everyone, whatever their sex, age, ability, race or ethnic group should be exposed to and shown participating in a variety of activities and roles.
- **foster curiosity, enjoyment and awareness of cultural differences and similarities.** Resources should be provided and activities undertaken which will broaden young people's knowledge and awareness of the world in which we live. Different religious festivals can be acknowledged or celebrated at appropriate times throughout the year.
- **enable young people to stand up for themselves against discriminatory behaviour.** People will only do this if they feel supported. A clearly defined and implemented anti-bullying policy agreed by all involved is an essential element of this type of support.
- **be committed to fairness and justice for all.**

Youth workers as role models

The adults are the single most important resource in any environment, as they have the power to structure the environment, allocate the budget, plan activities, organise the space or to share those responsibilities with the young people. If they are not aware of or committed to equality and diversity, then all the equipment and exciting activities in the world will be of little use. In other words, the success or failure of a programme committed to equality and diversity depends on the youth workers involved. Finally, it is imperative that youth work services draw up an equality policy and corresponding procedures.

References, resources and further reading

Devlin, M., 2006, *Inequality and the Stereotyping of Young People*, Dublin: The Equality Authority and the National Youth Council of Ireland.

Donohoe, J. and F. Gaynor, 2011, *Education and Care in the Early Years* (4th ed.), Dublin: Gill and Macmillan.

Lalor, K., de Roiste, A. and M. Devlin, 2007, *Young People in Contemporary Ireland*, Dublin: Gill and Macmillan.

The Equality Authority and PDST, 2011, *Spotlight on Stereotyping*, Dublin: The Equality Authority and Professional Development Service for Teachers.

City of Dublin Youth Service Board, *Essential Guidelines for Good Practice: Toolkit.* Dublin: CDYSB. The *Toolkit* on Equality and Diversity provides guidelines for planning, monitoring and evaluation of practices in the workplace. It also gives a comprehensive list of relevant legislation and a valuable guide to a range of other sources and resources.

Health and Well-being

On various forms filled out about young people, there is often a section called 'Health History' or 'Medical History'. If a young person has not had any major illness or surgery, that section will be marked 'none'. In truth, the assertion that a young person has enjoyed good physical and mental health all their lives is just as important as the list of illnesses and operations would be for another person. A young person's health is not just the absence of disease and illness, but it is also about their ability to respond to challenges both physical and mental, and to regain health and balance in their lives following a setback.

Health has many dimensions and involves:

- Mental Health – psychological and mental well-being; ability to function in society and meet the demands of everyday life.
- Physical Health – physical well-being, including fitness.
- Emotional Health – the ability to express emotions appropriately and maintain a balance between negative and positive emotions.
- Social Health – the ability to relate appropriately to other people in our society.
- Spiritual Health – to do with personal beliefs, values and morals; how a person may achieve peace and harmony in their lives; what values drive them and their inner life.

There are many factors that affect our health:

Socioeconomic determinants of health

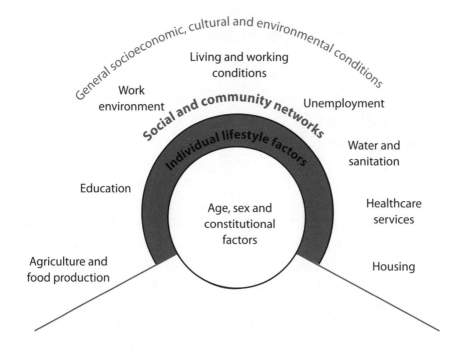

Many people blame a lack of services or the environment for poor health, but research suggests that the choices that we make are the biggest factor (53%) in the state of our health (Department of Health and Children, 2000). Of course, the choices that we make are influenced by a number of other factors such as family, social class, education, peer group, advertising, and much more. The next biggest influences on our health are sex, age and genetic factors. As outlined in Section 1, during adolescence different parts of the brain develop at different rates, and some of the latest to mature are the ones that help us to make well thought-out and logical decisions, resist impulses and deny our 'gut responses'.

It is important that youth services enable young people to assess their health, identify risks, positive factors, protective factors and resources available to them. Young people should be enabled to understand that everyone has ups and downs in life, but they should also be able to identify the risks – what might knock them off-balance, what their weak spots might be. Adopting an attitude of 'it won't happen to me' is not helpful. Young people should be able to identify the positive factors in their lives including their strengths, strong emotional ties especially if within the family, past successes in life and positive role models. Young people should be facilitated in finding out where to get help and support for health issues; these may include a school counsellor, or a youth worker ready and able to listen or expert services in the appropriate area.

Health service entitlements for young people

Children in Ireland are dependants of their parents and have the same entitlement to health services as their parents. This means that if your parents have a medical card, you are included as a dependant on that card and are entitled to the same range of services as your parents. Sixteen is the usual cut off point for child health services, but if the young person is in education they may continue to be included as a dependant on their parents up to the age of 25. Children may be regarded as dependants up to age 18 (or 23 if in full-time education) for the purposes of the *prescribed drugs and medicines* scheme; basically, this means that members of a family will be entitled to get their prescribed medicines free of charge after they have spent a certain amount in any one calendar month.

Children and young people in secondary schools are entitled to free screening and follow-up treatment free of charge if deemed necessary. The cut off age is 15 years.

Consent to medical treatment

In general, once children have reached the age of 16 years they can give consent for medical or surgical procedures for themselves and can consult with their GP without their parents' knowledge.

Mental health

'About 70% of health problems and most mortality among the young arise as a result of mental health difficulties and substance-use disorders' (McGorry, 2005). Almost 75% of all serious mental health difficulties first emerge between the ages of 15 and 25 (Hickie, 2004; Kessler et al, 2005; Kim-Cohen et al, 2003, reported in the executive summary of *My World Survey*, 2012.

According to *My World Survey* launched by Headstrong and the Department of Psychology at UCD in 2012, 'the number one health issue for young people is their mental health' (introduction, Executive Summary, p. vii). This report is based on research on about 15,000 young people across the country from all walks of life. The study found that the majority of young Irish people enjoy reasonably good mental health, but that when problems arise they emerge in early adolescence and peak in the late teens and early twenties. The study also found that gender affected both risk-taking and protective factors, but that for all, the adolescent period is particularly vulnerable.

The following themes were found to be significantly related to key mental health indicators, as measured by the MWS:

- 'One Good Adult' is important in the mental well-being of young people, i.e. having at least one supportive adult in their life.
- Excessive drinking has very negative consequences for the mental health and adjustment of young people.
- Young adults' experiences of financial stress are strongly related to their mental health and well-being.
- Rates of suicidal thoughts, self-harm and suicide attempts were found to be higher in young adults who did not seek help or talk about their problems.
- Talking about problems is associated with lower mental health distress and higher positive adjustment.

(*My World Survey* Executive summary, p. ix)

In the MWS a fifth of young people surveyed had engaged in self-harm at some stage and the mortality rate from suicide is the fourth highest in the EU for the 15–24 age group and the third highest among males in the 15–19 year age group (Eurostat, various years). Self-harming is highest for girls and suicide highest for boys.

Self-harm

Self-harm or self-injury is injuring oneself deliberately, usually on a regular basis; the most common methods are cutting, burning or poisoning. Mostly people who self-harm do so in order to cope with painful feelings associated with something that is happening or has happened in their lives. A common myth is that it is an attention-seeking device; in fact most young people who harm themselves hide not only the self-harm but also the fact that they are in distress at all. For a number of years in Ireland records have been kept on people who have presented for treatment following self-harm. The latest figures (for 2010) are presented in the *Report of the National Registry of Self-harm*. This report shows that numbers presenting for treatment are increasing; the gender gap is decreasing; and by far the most common method of self-harm was by drug overdose. Cutting was the next most common method, and although alcohol itself was rare as a sole method of self-harm, it was involved in two-fifths of all those treated (41%). Another significant and consistent finding is that self-harm is highest among young people.

People injure themselves as a way of:

- coping with overwhelming feelings.
- communicating when the young person cannot find the words or the way to explain their feelings.
- finding some relief.
- punishing themselves.
- gaining a sense of control over their lives.

Some warning signs of self-harm might be:

- unexplained injuries.
- a pattern of curious scars, scabs or abrasions on the arms and legs and a refusal or reluctance to explain these.
- sharp objects stored in strange places.
- wearing long-sleeved clothing in warm conditions.
- low self-esteem.
- being withdrawn or secretive.
- an inability to function at work or in school.
- depression and anxiety.
- self-harm can also be associated with substance use and excessive dieting.

How the youth worker can support people who self-injure

In general:

- Make it clear to all young people in your service at all times that you are prepared to listen to their problems and concerns in a caring, non-judgemental way.
- Encourage all young people to seek health and balance in their everyday lives.
- Make sure that the programme encourages young people to discuss issues, identify coping methods and to make positive changes in their lives.
- Try to remove any stigma or drama around self-harm by bringing the issue out into the open through discussion and group activities.

- Ensure that the service has policies and procedures in place around the issue of self-harm.

Specifically:
- Do not make false promises or promise to keep information secret.
- Avoid close examination of the injury or asking the young person for details of the injury – if it needs medical attention the person should be encouraged and supported in accessing such services.
- Remember, the young person has confided in you because they have decided they can trust you; you must act on that trust by acknowledging the issue and engaging with it.
- Try to give some control to the young person by discussing their options and helping them choose rather than taking over.
- Provide access to information and resources and support the young person in accessing them.
- Remember that the young person who self-harms is in need of attention, and do not dismiss their actions as attention-seeking.
- Monitor the reactions of the other young people and provide support and guidance so that that friends and peers can be enabled to be supportive.
- Although some people who self-harm may go on to attempt suicide, and every act of self-harm should be taken seriously, it is not a predictor of suicidal behaviour.

Suicide

Suicide is the act of intentionally causing one's own death. In 1993 suicide was decriminalised in Ireland. There are approximately 400 deaths from suicide each year in Ireland; it is the leading cause of premature death – much higher than road traffic accidents. Numbers also show that Ireland has the fifth-highest rate in the European Union. There is a gender gap, and the male to female ratio is 4:1. The peak age for men committing suicide is 20–24 years and for women is 50–54 years, but recently the greatest increase has been in the number of suicides by girls and young women in the 15–24 age group. An alarming statistic indeed is that four-fifths of young men know someone who has committed suicide. So, suicide is an issue that youth workers are going to come across in the course of their involvement with young people.

Suicide is associated with underlying mental health issues, interpersonal difficulties such as bullying and financial difficulties, but it must be remembered that some people commit suicide and it would not be obvious that any such issues were a factor.

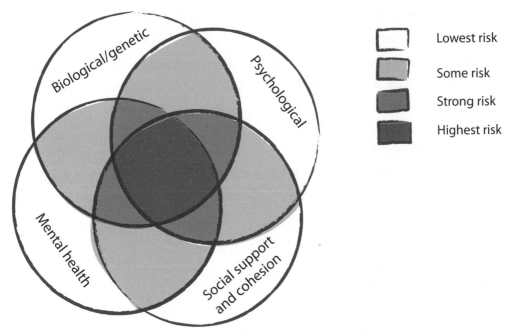

(Adapted from 'Reaching Out: Awareness Training on Suicide Prevention in Ireland', 2010, p. 13)

It can be difficult for those close to someone who has committed suicide to see any cause or warning signs, but for many there are identifiable triggers such as

- the end of a relationship
- death of someone close, particularly if by suicide
- divorce
- loss of employment
- financial difficulties
- isolation
- bullying
- … and more

The following may be warning signs that someone is thinking of committing suicide:
- giving away possessions – 'I won't be needing these anymore'
- withdrawal from school, family, club, activities

- loss of interest in people and hobbies
- substance abuse
- reckless behaviour – 'it doesn't matter'
- change in behaviour
- impulsivity in behaviour
- talking about suicide – may include throwaway remarks such as 'I wish I were dead'; 'everyone would be better off without me'; 'all my problems will soon be over' and so on.

The role of the youth worker

The difficult question a youth worker faces when they suspect a young person may have suicidal thoughts is what to do.

Key actions

- take the threat of suicide seriously
- be non-judgemental
- ask about their thoughts of suicide
- listen to their reasons for wanting to die
- listen to their reasons for living
- offer support but not false promises
- do not agree to keep their plan a secret
- stay with the person
- make a safe plan
- disable the suicide plan
- get professional help

For more information on any of the above, avail of professional advice such as ASIST (Applied Suicide Intervention Skills Training: see resources on p. 232).

Following a suicide

In the aftermath of a suicide, consider the needs of those in the immediate community, organisation or youth group, the family and friends and the wider community.

For the immediate community:

- Appoint a response team to include the person in charge, an outside counsellor and a spiritual advisor.
- Provide accurate information as soon as possible – this is the best way to combat the spread of rumours.
- A staff meeting is essential, and a statement should be prepared so that all staff members are saying the same thing to service users and the wider community. There should be a designated spokesperson.
- Young people should receive information in their familiar groups and settings if possible and from a familiar adult also.

Dealing with reactions:

Common reactions are shock, anger, guilt, fear and a sense of betrayal and rejection among others. Typical questions include a search to understand why the young person committed suicide and if anything could have been done anything to prevent it. Some people may be quiet, some may act out and some may want the normal programme of activities to go ahead.

- Encourage young people to talk about the person and the suicide after they have heard the news.
- Don't romanticise or glamorise the death in any way. Watch the words you use.
- Listen to feelings expressed and don't presume or tell people how you think they should feel.
- It is important that young people know that they are not responsible for the suicide through anything they did or didn't do or say.
- Let people know where they can access outside help and counselling.
- Let them know the funeral arrangements.

Remember:

Some people may use expressions of grief as a way of getting attention for themselves; recognise their needs but do not allow close friends of the young person to be sidelined by those seeking attention. Be mindful of the danger that those close to the deceased may themselves contemplate suicide as a way to stay close to their lost loved one or as an escape from their own painful feelings. Young people should be encouraged to go to the funeral and be involved in the ceremony if the family wish it.

As time passes, the strongest feelings of grief should subside, but for each young person this will be different. In the long term you should be concerned if a young person becomes very withdrawn or angry, does not get involved with friends and activities, or if they persist in talking about the death.

Mental health resources

There are quite a number of resources on the promotion of health and well-being and these should be part and parcel of the programme in any services aimed at young people. The National Youth Health Programme (www.youthhealth.ie), which is a partnership between the National Youth Council of Ireland, the HSE and the Department of Children and Youth Affairs has extensive material on all aspects of youth and health; training, workshops, bibliography and material for use in groups as well as links to other sites and to research.

Worksheets, resources for exploring different themes around health, self-harm and suicide are available from the NYCI and HSE and through the aforementioned National Health Promotion Unit.

The following list is merely the tip of iceberg in terms of the resources – information, worksheets and training that is available.

O'Sullivan, Rainsford and Sihera, 2011, *Suicide Prevention in the Community: A Practical Guide*. Available on *www.hse.ie*

This publication contains detailed guidelines and comprehensive information on nationwide resources along with case studies and guidance on policies and supports for all organisations from schools to sports clubs, self-help groups to individuals. Some of those listed below are also available in this guide.

'Good Habits of Mind' booklet

The National Youth Council of Ireland and the HSE have developed a booklet called 'Good Habits of Mind'. It is a mental health promotion resource for those working with young people in out-of-school settings. The booklet sets out guidelines for the youth organisation and their workers on how to promote positive mental health and policy development.

You can download a PDF of the 'Good Habits of Mind' booklet at: *http://www.youth.ie/nyci/good-habits-mind*

Headstrong

Headstrong was set up in response to a need to change the way Ireland thinks about youth mental health, so that young people are connected to their community and have the resilience to face challenges to their mental health. *www.headstrong.ie*

My World Survey gives a very good overall picture of issues in relation to mental health among the young people of Ireland today.

Pieta House

Pieta House is a Centre for the Prevention of Self-Harm or Suicide. Pieta House offers a counselling service for people who have tried to take their lives and also for people who have engaged in self-harming behaviours.

For further information phone (01) 601 0000 or go to: *www.pieta.ie*

Console

Console provides professional counselling, support and helpline services to those bereaved through suicide. It is a national organisation with Centres in Dublin, Galway, Limerick, Cork, Wexford and Kildare. Console's services include a 24-hour helpline for anyone bereaved by suicide, which aims to provide support, advice and referral services.

Console also provides individual and family counselling, therapy and support groups, and other suicide prevention and community awareness projects. For further information see *www.console.ie*.

ASIST

ASIST (Applied Suicide Intervention Skills Training) is a two-day interactive workshop in suicide first-aid. It is suitable for all kinds of caregivers – health workers, teachers, community workers, Gardaí, youth workers, volunteers, and the family, friends and co-workers of those at risk. These training workshops are co ordinated by Resource Officers for Suicide Prevention of the HSE. Support available and paper copies available from your local Resource Officer for Suicide Prevention. See *www.nosp.ie* for more details.

Available from www.winstonswish.org.uk:
Beyond the Rough Rock: Supporting a child who has been bereaved through suicide
This book offers practical advice for families and gives parents and professionals the confidence to involve children in discussions.

Muddles, Puddles & Sunshine
Activity book to remember someone who has died (for younger children).
Out of the Blue
For teenagers.

Available from the Irish Association of Suicidology:
Managing Grief and Loss after Suicide

Available from Barnardo's
Information pack: Bereavement
Death: Helping Teenagers' Understanding
Death: Helping Children's Understanding
Helping teenagers to cope with death
Coping with death for children aged 6 to 12
Coping with death for parents of children between 6 and 12
You Are Not Alone: Directory of Bereavement Support Services 2008

Available from www.nosp.ie
National Quality Standards for the Provision of Suicide Bereavement Services: A Practical Resource for Organisations

References, resources and further reading

The information and guidelines contained in this section were taken principally from the following sources:

Dooley, B. and A. Fitzgerald, 2012. *My World Survey: National Study of Mental Health in Ireland,* Dublin; Headstrong and UCD, 2011, *Suicide Prevention in the Community: A Practical Guide,* available from www.youthhealth.ie/sites/youthhealth.ie/files/Community Booklet Suicide-Prevention

National Registry of Deliberate Self-harm. Retrieved from www.nsrf.ie 4 June 2012

O'Sullivan, M., Rainsford, M. and N. Sihera, 2011, *Suicide Prevention in the Community: A Practical Guide.* Available on www.youthhealth.ie/sites/files/communitybookletsuicide_prevention/

Sexual Health

According to the World Health Organisation (WHO),

> Sexual health is a state of physical, mental and social well-being in relation to sexuality. It requires a positive and respectful approach to sexuality and sexual relationships, as well as the possibility of having pleasurable and safe sexual experiences, free of coercion, discrimination and violence.

Sexual health and well-being is a topic that should be introduced and delivered in a proactive way with young people. An Irish Study of Sexual Health and Relationships (ISSHR, 2006) states that in the role of sexual health knowledge 'accurate targeting of sexual health services and messages is imperative.' (p. 283). It was also suggested that providing sexual health guidance on a regular basis to both men and women greatly improves the consistent use of condoms and thus reduces the levels of crisis pregnancy and sexually transmitted infections.

This advice and guidance should be offered at home, school and in the youth centres. All adults working with young people must also be aware that the age of consent for sexual intercourse for heterosexual and homosexual sex is 17 for boys and girls.

What is an STI?

A sexually transmitted infection (STI) is an infection that can be passed from one person to another through vaginal sexual intercourse or skin-to-skin contact (vaginal, anal or oral). One or both sexual partners must be infected in order for the infection to spread. The most common STIs are as follows:

Chlamydia

Anogenital Warts

Gonorrhoea

Genital Herpes

Human Immunodeficiency Virus (HIV)

Syphilis

Trichomoniasis

Hepatitis B

Hepatitis C

Pubic Lice

What are the symptoms of an STI?

- Unpleasant and unusual vaginal or penile discharge
- Lumps, sores or ulcers on the genitals
- Pain when passing urine
- Pelvic pain
- Itching in the pubic/genital area
- Unusual pain during intercourse

Alarmingly, STIs can have no symptoms at all, and even if they have no symptoms, they remain contagious. Therefore, young people who are sexually active must go for regular STI screenings. To be sexually active means vaginal, oral and/or anal sex.

STI facts that young people need to know

- Many young people in Ireland have an STI without realising it. As stated earlier, some people have no symptoms indicating that they have an STI, and therefore if they continue to have sexual relationships, they will spread the infection. If chlamydia is not treated, it can cause infertility in women.
- It is possible to have more than one STI at a time.
- You can get an STI the first time that you engage in sexual activity.
- STI can be spread without having 'full sex'.
- Condoms reduce the risk of spreading or contracting an infection.
- Vaginal, oral and anal sex should be avoided until the STI has cleared.
- If a woman has genital herpes when having a baby she may have to have a caesarean section.

STIs are all treated differently depending on the type of infection. Please see table below.

Table 4.3.1 STI treatments

STI	Type of Infection	Treatment
Chlamydia, syphilis and gonorrhoea	Bacterial	Antibiotics
Warts	Viral	Solutions to burn, freeze or dry off
Pubic lice and scabies	Infestations	Lotions
Herpes	Viral	Treatments can help relieve some of the symptoms
HIV	Viral	No cure but effective treatments are available

Think about...

... a 2009 survey of men and women, aged 20–29.
Of the group surveyed, 51.7% were male, 47.1% were female.
Total number treated for: STIs 10,834.
Chlamydia and trichomoniasis accounted for half of all STIs diagnosed; anogenital warts accounted for a quarter.

A 2010 survey of men and women, aged 20–29.
Total number of people treated for STIs: 12,162.
Chlamydia was the most common STI, accounting for half of all diagnoses; it is reckoned to be underreported by 70%.
Anogenital warts account for a quarter of diagnoses.
Incidences of gonorrhoea (636) and herpes simplex (896) have doubled since 2009.

(www.hpsc.ie)

Young people should realise that having enjoyable and healthy sex is an important part of life for many people. People who are young, old, middle-aged, heterosexual, gay, lesbian or bisexual have sexual relationships, and each person must take responsibility for looking after their own sexual health in order to have an enjoyable sexual relationship with their partner.

What support can youth workers offer?

- Information, talks and interactive workshops should be designed by the youth workers or could be a topic for a peer education programme.
- Quizzes and polls about sexuality and sexual health can be given to the young people in the youth centre. (See below for resources.)
- Youth workers should promote healthy and supportive conversations with young people about sex, sexual health and sexuality.
- Youth workers need to encourage other adults to get involved in sexual health awareness including parents, family members, teachers, fellow colleagues – all the key people who may have an influence on the young person.
- Youth workers should ensure that young people are supported in terms of having someone to talk to and make sense of all the mixed messages that are out there.
- Youth worker should also inform young people about resources and where to find factual information that is easy to understand.

References, resources and further reading

www.sexualhealth.ie
www.spunout.ie
www.b4udecide.ie
www.healthpromotion.ie
www.crisispregnancy.ie
www.thinkcontraception.ie
www.belongto.ie
Local health personnel may be available to run workshops.

 Activity:

Go to some of the online resources mentioned above; find some questionnaires and activities that could be used or adapted for use in the youth service.

Substance Use and Misuse

Categories of drugs
Facts and figures
National Drugs Strategy 2009–2016
Principles of good practice
Indicators of substance use
Confidentiality
Sample drug incident template

The use and misuse of substances is a complex area and provides many challenges and dilemmas for the youth workers. This section will endeavour to provide basic information and guidelines of good practice; finally additional resources will be signposted to enable further exploration of the area.

Categories of drugs

Substances, commonly referred to as drugs are divided into four categories:

- Legal drugs – alcohol and cigarettes.
- Illegal drugs – divided into different types: stimulants, narcotics, solvents, headshop drugs, hallucinogens and opiates.
- Prescriptive drugs – what the doctor prescribes and are then dispensed by the pharmacy.
- Over-the-counter drugs – can be accessed and bought freely either in pharmacies or supermarkets and other shops.

Within these four categories there are several hundred types of drugs, many of them freely available to young people

Taking substances, regardless of category, affects both body and mind. While there is lots of concern for young people being exposed to illegal drugs, Crosscare would say that the 'most harm and the greatest risk comes from legal drugs such as alcohol, cigarettes and the inappropriate use of medicines' (2010, p. 6). For young people, risk-taking and pushing boundaries is part of growing up, and many youth workers have first-hand experience of how drugs (whether legal or illegal) have an impact on the young people who attend their services.

Facts and figures

The National Documentation Centre on Drug Use shows that cannabis is the most widely used drug in Europe (estimated 78 million users) by people between the ages of 15 and 64 years.

It is estimated that about 14.5 million Europeans have used cocaine at least once in their lives, on average 4.3% of adults aged 15–64 years.

In Ireland, a survey in 2010/11 of 7,669 people (4,967 in Ireland and 2,002 in Northern Ireland) aged between 15 and 64 years old show that over one in four people had used cannabis, making it the most commonly used illegal drug in Ireland and 6.8% had tried cocaine at least once.

A report from Crosscare 2010 states that per annum:
- Nicotine in the form of cigarettes leads to about 5,000 deaths in Ireland
- Alcohol leads to 1,000 deaths
- Heroin leads to about 100 deaths

National Drugs Strategy 2009–2016

The overall objective of the National Drugs Strategy is to continue to tackle the harm caused to individuals and society by the misuse of drugs through a concerted focus on the five pillars:
- reduction
- prevention
- treatment
- rehabilitation
- research

The aims of the Strategy are to:
- create a safer society through the reduction of the supply and availability of drugs for illicit use;

- minimise problem drug use throughout society;
- provide appropriate and timely substance treatment and rehabilitation services (including harm reduction services) tailored to individual needs;
- ensure the availability of accurate, timely, relevant and comparable data on the extent and nature of problem substance use in Ireland;
- have in place an efficient and effective framework for implementing the National Substance Misuse Strategy 2009–2016.

Principles of good practice

The following list outlines some principles of good practice, which should be borne in mind when youth workers are undertaking work with young people in relation to substances.

It is essential that workers recognise that work around drugs issues with all young people is part of good youth work practice.

- Work should be undertaken with all young people and not just targeted at those young people who are believed to be involved in drug use. The only exception to this should be in the case of a project funded to work with a specific cohort of young people.
- The process should not be different to any other youth work practice.
- A wide definition of the word 'drugs' must be used.
- Workers should recognise the harmful effects of stereotyping young people involved in drug use.
- Non-judgemental approaches are essential. Workers should not condone the use of drugs but equally should not condemn young people who use drugs.
- The importance of peer groups must be recognised and workers should encourage positive peer group support.
- Workers must accept that risk-taking is an important part of development and that for many young people this may include legal and illegal substance use.
- Workers should be prepared to support all young people and offer advocacy. If individuals feel unable to offer sufficient support, young people should be advised about appropriate specialist agencies.
- Workers should promote the self-esteem and confidence of young people. Young people must not be perceived as their actions e.g., drug user, but as important valuable individuals.

- Workers must respect the decisions made by young people and aim to ensure their health and well-being.

(Bissett, 2010, p. 10)

Indicators of substance use

There are warning signs that a young person may have begun to use substances which may be cause for concern:

School and family	Lots of days absent from school Losing interest in school/youth centre/family Low grades Absences from extracurricular activities Withdrawn from family and friends, keeping secrets Irresponsible with school work or family/personal possessions Argumentative
Social and emotional	Changing appearance of hair, dress, clothes, etc., and possibly a change in music taste Low self-esteem and self-confidence Sad, depressed, withdrawn from their friends, keeping secrets Mood swings and irritable
Physical	Tiredness Persistent cough or health problems Red and glassy eyes Lip chewing

* It is important not to jump to conclusions too quickly, but youth workers should be open to the possibility that a young person exhibiting some of these symptoms has begun to use substances.

What to do if a young person comes to the youth service under the influence of illegal substances

The first thing that must be done is to assess whether the person is at risk to themselves or to others in the youth centre. The person is at risk if they are abusive or threatening towards the young people in the service and/or the youth workers.

Not at risk	At risk
Try not to panic – speak slowly and try not to show anxiety	Do not admit access Ring their parents
Explain that what they are feeling will pass	Ring an ambulance Direct all other members of the youth centre to an activity
Encourage them to settle in a quiet calm room, dim the lights. If they start breathing quickly, calm them down and ask them to take long, deep breaths	
Don't allow them to over-exert themselves.	
Don't leave them alone	

(Adapted from *www.dap.ie* and Youth Work Ireland)

Confidentiality

Confidentiality involves keeping information given by or about an individual private. It is fundamental to good working relationships in a youth work setting. First and foremost, youth workers have a duty of care to protect the young person attending the service and therefore have to act or report any such issues that arise including taking drugs whether they are legal, illegal, prescribed or over-the-counter drugs.

The following are the guidelines in relation to confidentiality published by Youth Work Ireland (2012):

Given the nature of youth work, those working with young people may find themselves in a position where young people disclose sensitive information about personal issues. It is particularly important not to promise complete confidentiality before knowing what a young person is going to say, as it may be necessary to share that information with others.
The worker should clarify that there are limits to confidentiality between the worker and the young person or group. This means that the worker will have to take any disclosed information about risks to anyone's safety or possible legal actions further.
Whilst confidentiality is important the young person should know that if it becomes necessary for health and safety or legal reasons or Duty of Care requirements for the worker to speak to a third party, contact might be made without their consent. In every case the welfare of the young person concerned must be a primary consideration.
In working with drug users, workers must maintain a balance between the requirements of the law and the interests of the individual with whom they are working. The nature of the relationship offered by the worker should be made clear from the start in order that there be a clear understanding between worker and 'client'.
In such an understanding the drug user would know that, usually, the worker is not required, in law, to inform anyone that a person has used solvents, an illegal drug, or is in possession of illegal drugs. It should be made clear that the worker would speak to a third party if it were felt to be in the interests of the welfare of the person concerned, although this would not take place without their prior knowledge.
Within this understanding the worker should encourage the young person to make their own choices about how they deal with drug-related problems and should support and encourage the young person in any positive decisions they take.
Habitual drug users should be encouraged to use the support and services of appropriate agencies such as local HSE services, treatment and addiction services, counselling services, etc.
Recording and maintenance of incidents will respect the rights of young people to confidentiality where appropriate.

(Bissett, 2010, p. 23)

Sample Drug Incident Template

When did the incident occur?

Where did the incident occur?

Who was present?

What exactly occurred? (A separate account should be recorded for each person who witnessed the incident.)

Who was/were the on-site worker(s)/volunteer(s)?

How was the situation handled?

Were the organisation's agreed procedures followed during and after the incident? If not, why not?

What will be the organisation's formal response/follow-up, if any?

Were any external agencies/individuals contacted or involved? If yes, how?

Will there be any follow-up required with any external agencies/individuals who were contacted or involved?

Signed _____ Manager _____ Date _____

References, resources and further reading

Bissett, F., 2010, *Dealing with Drugs, Alcohol and Tobacco in Youth Work Settings. Guidelines for Youth Workers*, Dublin: Youth Work Press

Copping On programme

National Advisory Committee on Drugs

Parachute programme

Public Health Information and Research Branch

www.dap.ie

www.dhsspsni.gov.uk

www.drugs.ie

www.nacd.ie

www.spunout.ie

Youth Homelessness

Homelessness in Irish law

Like adults, young people become homeless for a variety of reasons. Youth homelessness wasn't really recognised as a problem until the 1990s although various voluntary organisations had been providing services for homeless young people for decades prior to then. A basic timeline of relevant legislation and developments to do with youth homelessness is as follows:

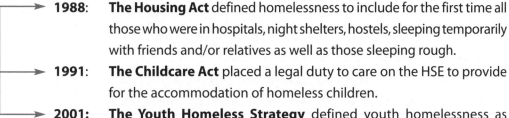

1988: **The Housing Act** defined homelessness to include for the first time all those who were in hospitals, night shelters, hostels, sleeping temporarily with friends and/or relatives as well as those sleeping rough.

1991: **The Childcare Act** placed a legal duty to care on the HSE to provide for the accommodation of homeless children.

2001: **The Youth Homeless Strategy** defined youth homelessness as anyone under 18 (but in certain circumstances under 21) who is

- sleeping rough
- sleeping anywhere not intended for night-time accommodation or not providing protection from the elements
- sleeping in temporary accommodation (hostels, shelters, bed and breakfasts) that provides protection from the elements but lacks other characteristics of a home or is only meant for the short term.
- sleeping in the homes of relatives or friends because they cannot go home.

The term more often used now is 'Out of Home' which at least recognises that there are underlying problems; the young person may have a 'home' but cannot live there.

Homelessness is largely an urban phenomenon exacerbated by the fact that young rural people who are out of home tend to gravitate towards urban areas.

Factors leading to homelessness

A study 'Pathways into Homelessness' (Maycock and Vekic, 2006) concluded that although there are many and varied reasons why young people become homeless, there are three factors that recur:

- a history of being 'in care' whether foster care or residential. Focus Point and Father Peter McVerry, both of whom provide homeless services for young people, highlight this factor also. Robinson (2008) suggests that up to a half of young homeless people have been in public care of some sort. The aftercare service or lack of it lets down our most vulnerable young people although the HSE is mandated to provide aftercare services up to age 21 years under the Childcare Act 1991. The Youth Work Act 2001 and the National Children's Strategy are also relevant to this issue. 'Out of care' also may include those who have been hospitalised or in detention centres for long periods.
- household instability and family conflict, domestic violence, marital break-down, parental substance use, ongoing child abuse and neglect all figure prominently among the factors which drive young people away from home.
- negative peer behaviour and associated problem behaviour. Such issues are usually related to family issues as noted above.

In contemporary Ireland, unaccompanied minors and young people who are trafficked can be added to the list of those at risk of homelessness.

Definitive figures in relation to numbers of young people who are homeless are difficult to access. *Counted In* (Homeless Agency, 2008) estimated that there were 567 children homeless with their families, and the latest HSE figures found 234 unattached children who were homeless. It is thought that many children and young adults do not contact any services because they fear being returned to abusive and intolerable situations. That the numbers have increased greatly in recent years seems supported by media reports on increased pressure on services aimed at these young people such as Focus Point and the Peter McVerry Trust.

Effects of homelessness

- Isolation from family and sources of support.
- Discrimination – many young homeless people mention the fact that the public treat you like you are 'scum', 'don't trust you' and 'see you as useless'. They are called names, beaten and worse on a regular basis.
- Vulnerable to exploitation – to prostitution, drug and alcohol abuse in their efforts to cope.
- Health deterioration both physical and mental – obviously a problem for those who are sleeping rough, but those who are constantly moving around and looking for a bed for the night are also under enormous physical and psychological pressure.
- Uncertainty and instability – nothing to look forward to; many people who are homeless over long periods say they lose a sense of their own history, that they have neither a past nor a future.
- Constant surveillance – in hostels, by the Gardaí, shopkeepers, etc.
- Low self-esteem – as a result of a combination of all the reasons that they became homeless and the factors mentioned here. As outlined in the chapter on adolescence, this period in a person's life is crucial in developing self-identity and self-concept. Young people out of home are particularly vulnerable and less likely to be able to access support.
- Lack of privacy and lack of personal possessions.
- Physical and sexual victimisation.
- Lack of access to services because they have no fixed address.
- Stable relationships are more difficult to form and to keep, both because of a lack of trust but also because the person who is homeless tends to be transient.
- Difficulty obtaining or holding onto employment.
- Acculturation – the younger and the longer a young person is homeless, the more acclimatised to street life and living on their wits they become; intervention and rehabilitation become more and more difficult. Getting involved in criminal activity, intimidation, violence and substance abuse can become a routine in a desperate bid to survive.

However there are many young people in this situation who are highly motivated to change, and given the right support and services they can get their lives together. Case histories from the Peter McVerry Trust, Simon Community and Focus Point are testament to this. Youth services can also be a place of refuge, advice, support and guidance.

Homeless services

The HSE is mandated to provide suitable accommodation for all young persons under 18 years. The HSE is also mandated to provide for those who are in 'after-care' situations.

If over 18 years, a young person can apply to be housed by their local authority. The Housing Welfare Officer is the person responsible for dealing with applications in any local authority. In effect because of an under supply of social housing, young single people who have no children may come way down the list and will be offered hostel or B&B accommodation.

In Dublin, the Dublin Region Homeless Executive is responsible for the coordination of services. Numerous voluntary bodies provide accommodation and associated services and several are listed below.

EPIC Empowering People in Care: www.epiconline.ie

Local Youth Information Centres: www.youthinformation.ie

Focus Ireland has a directory of homeless services for each province: www.focusireland.ie

The HSE has a Homeless Persons Unit, one for men and one for women and children and provides information and support throughout the country: www.hse.ie

The Simon Community provides services for adults throughout the country: www.simon.ie

Crosscare is a social care agency of the Dublin Archdiocese that offers various services to homeless young people in the greater Dublin area: www.crosscare.ie

The Salvation Army offers services to homeless people and also offers a service to family members who have lost contact with each other: www.salvationarmy.ie

The Peter McVerry Trust (formerly the Arrupe Society) offers various services, but particularly services to young people who are under 18 years old and homeless: www.pmvtrust.ie

The Homeless Agency: www.homelessagency.ie

Threshold: www.threshold.ie

References, resources and further reading

Robinson, P., 2008, *Working with Young Homeless People*, London: Jessica Kingsley.

Maycock, P. and Vekic, K., 2006, *Understanding Youth Homelessness in Dublin City: Key findings from the first phase of a longitudinal cohort study.* Dublin: Stationery Office.

Pillinger, J., 2006, *Preventing homelessness: a comprehensive preventative strategy to prevent homelessness in Dublin, 2005–2010.* Dublin: Homeless Agency.

McVerry, Peter, 2003, *The Meaning is in the Shadows.* Dublin: Veritas.

The Homeless Agency, 2008, *Counted In.* Dublin.

Information Technology and Social Media

Adolescence, IT and social media
The positives and negatives of social media
Good practice for IT and social media in youth work

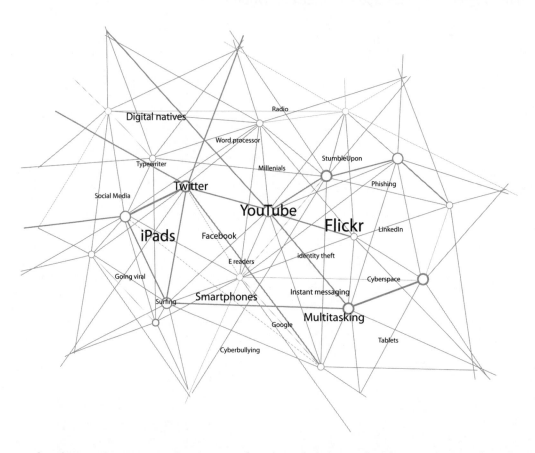

Each advance in communications technology has brought about its own changes and challenges for society. The development and rapid adoption of the Internet at the end of the 20th century has left us in a situation where the Internet is a part of everyone's life but we still do not fully understand its advantages and disadvantages. In many countries, including Ireland, governments have supported and encouraged Internet use because of its value to young and old for learning and communication.

Before the Internet, mass communications were 'top down' or 'one to many'; millions of people might see the same film in the cinema, but very few of them would ever produce one of their own. Today, the Internet allows for 'many-to-many' communication. Now someone anywhere in the world can make a film, distribute it through video sites on the Internet and promote it through social networking sites and blogs.

As well as a forum for sharing your ideas with millions of people worldwide, the Internet is also a dominant tool for one-to-one communications through email, instant messaging, chat rooms, forums and social networks. Most anxieties about the Internet focus on the vulnerabilities of young people using the Internet for 'private' communication in this way.

Adolescence, IT and social media

Adolescents today grew up at a time when the Internet was widespread, and as such are often described as 'digital natives'. For this generation, the idea of instant communication with a person on the other side of the world is not extraordinary; 'virtual reality' is as valid and comfortable to them as the real world. Many young people use social media as a means of making new friends or for keeping in touch with family and friends as well as for a wide array of other activities like education, e-mail, gaming, keeping up with current affairs and celebrity gossip, viewing videos, downloading music and uploading pictures.

There are diverse views on whether IT and social media are good or bad for adolescents. Some people argue that the willingness of digital natives to immerse themselves in an online world is detrimental to their real-world development, mental health and social relationships. Others argue that young people online do the same things that young people have always done (or wanted to do) but in new, easier ways. As adolescence is a time when people begin to explore their identity and when their peers become very important, social media presents many positive opportunities but also plenty of negatives. Effects of Internet use on young people can be both positive and negative.

The positives and negatives of IT and social media

Positives:

The Internet can facilitate a wider social circle; therefore people with unusual hobbies and specialist interests can easily find like-minded people with whom to share and develop their interest.

- It is easier to keep in touch online with friends or family who live far away.
- Young people can create and disseminate their own material, whether writing blogs or posting their guitar playing on YouTube, and receive feedback. They can get involved in bigger projects or simply use the Internet as an audience for their own creativity; it is empowering.
- Young people can access new and broader sources of information at little cost.
- Online interaction enables individuals to explore their own and others' identities and to engage with particular subcultures.
- Young people who use the Internet regularly may develop a broad range of abilities including better multitasking, decision-making, research and typing skills. It increases their familiarity with technology and terminology that they may need for education and employment.
- A young person who has a problem can access support outside and information from outside their friends, family and locality if they so wish.
- The Internet can allow those who might otherwise be marginalised – for example those with limited mobility – to socialise and get involved with their peers.
- Online interaction increases economic, market and employment opportunities by creating wider circles in which to buy and sell goods and services and search for opportunities.
- Being online allows many people the chance to work from home.
- The Internet offers wider opportunities for education through online courses, free and paid.

Negatives:

- Many people using the Internet do not realise that it is not as personal or as private as it seems. The Internet's memory is potentially eternal and nothing on it is ever completely private. Whether people communicate on social networks or forums, upload videos or write blogs they are essentially performing to a worldwide audience with no way of knowing who may be watching.
- Internet marketing is huge business, and Internet advertising is more insidious and aggressive than it is in traditional media. Advertisers can easily gain access to personal information and tailor their campaigns accordingly.

- Research suggests that the technology we use affects how we think and even the way the neural pathways in our brain are formed. People who spend many hours a day on the Internet may find their critical thinking and ability to concentrate on single tasks for a long period of time is affected. For young people in school this has serious implications for study and sitting exams.
- Internet use can have a detrimental effect on family life due to long hours spent online and not with the family, and also because of conflicts arising from disagreements over the use, location and control of a computer.
- Cyberbullying is a constant threat and difficult for the victim to avoid. Bullying has been identified by youth workers and young people as one of the most worrying aspects of social networking.
- Access to violent and pornographic material is greater than ever before and is thought to have an effect on tolerance levels of same in some individuals.
- The risk of abuse and exploitation or grooming is increased. Many young people have their social media profiles set to 'public' so they are available for everyone to see. Because of the anonymity of the online world, sexual predators can easily disguise their identity and pose as someone of a different age or gender.
- Some people may become addicted to social media sites or games.
- Internet access creates another level of inequality between those who have good Internet connections and computer access and can avail of all the advantages listed above and those who do not for economic reasons or a lack of broadband availability.

Good practice for IT and social media in youth work

Though it may be a matter of time before we come to fully understand the implications of the Internet on the lives of young people, one things is certain: these new technologies and networks are here to stay and will continue to evolve. Young people, youth workers and youth services must be aware of the issues and seek to constantly evolve policies and management around IT and social media.

Davies and Cranston (2008) suggest that services should work through the following checklist in order to optimise the opportunities and minimise the risks offered by IT and social networking sites:

1 Survey – identify current access, engagement, skills and resources of both staff and young people; this will give a picture of the diverse skills that are available as well as a picture of the different uses that are made of IT and social media.

2 Safety – consider the implications for staff and young people, work on a policy and work together to minimise risk. See end of chapter for suggested resources.

3 Skills – ensure that staff members have the opportunity to learn skills and, in view of constant changes in IT and social media, to upgrade those skills regularly; in a word, training.

4 Strategy – explore opportunities to take advantage of these media to enhance youth work activities including marketing and advertising the service, communicating with members, providing links to supportive and information services; enabling and encouraging young people to be creative and/or get involved in wider socio-political issues.

By and large, although online communication and networking is facilitated by new and ever-changing technology which brings with it fresh opportunities and risks, the youth worker's approach should be informed by best practice. Some of the existing principles of best practice can easily be adapted to suit online concerns. For example, in relation to boundaries, in maintaining a professional relationship, youth workers should not be friends with young people who attend the service either in the real or the online world.

References, resources and further reading

Davies, T. and Cranston, P., 2008, *Youth Work and Social Networking: Final Research Report*, Funded by the National Youth Agency. Provides constructive guidelines for a proactive and positive approach that might be taken by youth workers and youth services. Available on
http://www.practicalparticipation.co.uk/publications/ Accessed June 2012.

Office for Internet Safety, 2008, *Get With It: A Parent's Guide to Social Networking Sites*, Dublin. A useful booklet that gives some ideas about areas which could be used in group discussions in a youth work setting. There are also a number of other useful publications on the site. Available from *www.internetsafety.ie.*

Introduction to Social Media for Youth Workers is a very basic introduction available from *http://www.slideshare.net/small/intro-to-social-media-for-youth-workers* Accessed June 2012

ENISA, 2011, *Cyber-Bullying and Online Grooming: helping to protect against the risks* European Network and Information Security Agency *http://www.enisa.europa.eu*

5

Doing Assignments and Research Projects

This section informs the reader about doing assignments and research projects. It takes the reader through the process of reading a brief, extracting key areas, putting the assignment together and presenting the findings. It also includes research methods and how to reference correctly. Examples of referencing from a number of sources are given and a bibliography is also explained.

There is also an excellent glossary of terms that are not only useful when doing assignment work but they will help you at examination time when questions are often phrased with words like, analyse, outline, discuss, etc.

Guidelines for preparing work for assessment

Getting the marks
Writing up an assignment
Doing a research project
Using the library
Research methods
Presentation of findings
Appendices
References and bibliography
Glossary of terms

Getting the marks

A common question asked by students when they are first given an assignment is 'Where do I start?' It is a very good question – and a very easy one to answer. First you must read the assignment brief carefully. Figure out what you are being asked to do (the words of the brief) and how you are expected to do it (the marking sheet).

For example, consider the following brief:

Present a comprehensive organisational profile that shows your understanding of the role of the youth worker and the community context of youth work.

The three key phrases here are 'organisational profile', 'role of youth worker', 'community context of youth work'.

Next, look at what you are being asked to do. In this instance it is to 'present a comprehensive profile' and 'show your understanding'.

The next task is to look at the marking sheet. Marking sheets can be found at the end of the component descriptor on the FETAC website. For example, for the above assignment, 15 marks went for the presentation of a comprehensive profile, which included: describe the community context; the structure; decision-making process; funding; and how the organisation responds to the needs of young people. So now you know what is required by the word 'comprehensive'!

The next step is to read and research – in other words, do some study. For the above assignment you might look at the website of the organisation and any annual reports, submissions, funding applications and promotional material they might have. You also have a look at the needs of young people generally – look to your textbooks for that, and to find out about the needs of young people in this particular community, look to newspaper reports and again back to reports and brochures from the organisation.

Then move on and focus on the other key words. If you are required to do primary research you might visit the organisation, or do a work experience placement there, interview the manager and workers, observe activities, talk to young people involved, etc. (A word of caution: you will need permission to interview any young people under 18 years, and they must not be identified in your assignment for reasons of privacy and confidentiality.)

Writing up an assignment

Your assignment will contain the following sections:

Title page and contents page

A contents page should indicate the relevant page numbers, and it goes without saying that you should then number your pages to correspond. In a short assignment there may be no need for a contents page.

Introduction

The brief that you get for the assignment can often be used as a guide for the introduction. Your introduction should be

  i) brief and clear;
 ii) it should give a broad overview of what you are going to cover in the essay/project, etc.; and
iii) it should include some general background information; how many young people, what age, what are the particular issues that will be examined.

Example: This assignment/essay/project provides information regarding the structure, funding and staffing of service X. It will examine the role of the youth worker in a community where there are high number of disadvantaged young people. Primary research will include X, Y and Z. An evaluation of the effectiveness of the service will be undertaken and recommendations made.

Aim and objectives

Not all assignments will require these to be written down, but it is a good mental exercise in order to get started. There is an old proverb that says, 'if you don't know where you're going, any road will take you there'. So to use that proverb; your aim is *where* you want to get to by the end of the day, and the objective is to *learn how* to read maps and to find out what roads will get you there by the most appropriate route.

Example: The aim is to complete an appropriate, enjoyable and worthwhile outdoor activity with the group of young people who come to the centre.

The objectives are to

- learn what might be appropriate to the stage of development or needs of the age group by matching theory to practice
- figure out what you need to do beforehand by learning what is involved in planning
- understand what makes for a worthwhile activity through reflection, evaluation and analysis.

Methodology

Again, this might only be relevant to a larger project or for an assignment that involves some research.

Your methodology is the way you got your information, and breaks down into primary and secondary research.

Primary or first-hand research methodologies include questionnaires, surveys, observations and case studies. Other relevant details include your sample size (if more than a single case study) and details on how you carried out your observations, etc.

See below for more detail on primary research methods. Secondary research involves reading others' primary research, mainly through reading text books, newspapers, websites, etc.

Content

This is the main part of your assignment, and there are no hard and fast rules, but you should first present your facts and figures. Brainstorm all the ideas that you think you might like to cover. Connect them to your introduction, which in turn is connected to the brief. Decide on a structure: each paragraph should deal with one topic or question. If we go back to the brief given in the example above, you might plan the following paragraphs:

- A brief description of the community in which the service operates
- The internal structure and staffing
- The numbers and characteristics (age, gender, etc.) of young people who attend the service
- A brief description of the programmes available
- Funding
- The needs of young people
- The role of the youth worker in the service
- The results of any primary research

Next, **analyse, criticise, evaluate, relate to theory, discuss, compare and make recommendations**. Again, what you do should be guided by the brief and the marking sheet. See glossary of terms below for further explanation.

Conclusion

In your conclusion, you should **summarize** your findings, **clarify** what you found and make **recommendations** based on your work. In simple language, *what was I looking for, what did I find and what does it mean?*

Set out your main points, but do not go into long repetitions of what you have already said. It is good to look again at the key terms and tasks that were set out in the brief. Do not be tempted either to include opinions and hunches here that were not evident in your research; do not introduce any new information in the conclusion. Finally, look to the future, or pose a question.

Going back to the original profile given in the example, you might conclude:

> This assignment found that although the structure and organisation were effective and youth workers trained and committed, cutbacks in funding were affecting programmes and rising unemployment in the area mean that more and more young people in the community have nothing to do. Therefore, the demands on youth work will become too great, the youth will suffer and the whole community may reap the effects of this in increasing social and psychological problems in the future.

References and bibliography

All written work must contain details of what you referred to – your references – and a bibliography of any work you read in preparation for writing. Details of how to write references and a bibliography appear on p. 268.

Doing a research project

Choosing a topic

To choose your topic, begin by listing your areas of interest. The final choice should be an individual one. If a group undertakes a project together, careful planning, close cooperation and regular reviews are required. Also, it is important in the introduction to clearly outline the role and tasks undertaken by each member of the group.

Narrowing the subject area

Inevitably, whether you are doing a school project or a Ph.D., you will begin with a broad idea, which then has to be narrowed down. For example, you might be interested in considering the impact of computer use on young people; the following questions would help to narrow the focus of the topic.

- Which aspects am I going to consider? Gaming, social media, learning programmes...
- What age group will I focus on? There will be a vast difference between the content of a study that has 12–13-year-olds rather than 20-year-olds as its focus.
- What approach will you take?
  - Effects of violence
  - Effects on general knowledge
  - Effects on social interaction
  - Effects on literacy

Statement of subject chosen

Write down a broad outline of the topic you are going to cover, your aims and your hypotheses.

Identify your sources:

- Where and how you are going to get your information? Be realistic. Start with your textbooks (secondary research). List all other possible sources: local libraries, facilities, services, newspapers, TV, local representatives, teachers, other students, staff at your work placement, young people.
- Do not just explore the material on the Internet. There is a wealth of information to be found online, but sometimes if you do not type in a certain key word, then you will miss out on one whole aspect. On the other hand, if you are browsing in the library or through a book, even the contents page may suggest approaches and ideas to you that you can then research further online.
- Do not be discouraged if there appears to be a lack of secondary material on your chosen topic. If there is very little already, then your project will be all the more interesting.

Using the library

In a library, it is useful to be familiar with the arrangements and divisions. All libraries are divided into three main areas

- Fiction: usually arranged by author in alphabetical order; it may also be sub-divided into different categories e.g. romance, adventure, science fiction, etc.
- Non-fiction: usually arranged by subject matter e.g. history, travel, etc.
- Reference: dictionaries, thesauri, journals, encyclopedias, etc.

All Irish libraries now use a computerised catalogue and you will be shown how to locate the books on this system. If you know the name of the book or the author, you can locate it using the author or subject index. If a particular title is not available in the library, the librarian will be able to tell in which library it is available.

When you have located a book, use the following approach to find out if it contains material that might be relevant or useful in your research. Check the

- contents page
- date of publication
- introduction
- conclusion
- index

Research methods

As already mentioned, there are two types of research, primary and secondary. Primary research covers all sources that the researcher has found out first-hand, and includes surveys, questionnaires, case study, checklist, interview, qualitative and quantitative research. Secondary research covers all sources studied towards the assignment, such as books, programmes, journals and websites.

If you are going to do primary research, decide what primary method suits your purpose.

Surveys

Surveys gain information from a selection of the population. Questionnaires, interviews or checklists are common tools for surveys. If you are going to use a questionnaire/interview or checklist, consider:

- What questions will you ask?
- How many people will be included in your research, and how will you select them?
- Are you going to approach organizations?
- How much is it going to cost?
- How much time will you need?

Table 5.1.1 Designing and using a questionnaire

Decide	what information do you want.
Design	what questions will help to obtain that information.
Write	the questions down in logical sequence on a 'form'.
Select	the people that you are going to question.
Ask	the questions to these people.
Record	the answers in as much detail as possible.
Analyse	the answers, using tick boxes, graphs or other suitable visuals that make them easy to read.
Present	the findings in an appropriate way.

Further primary research methods

- Case study – a detailed profile of a person, group, organization or even a country, usually used to illustrate a point of view or a theory.
- Checklist – a list that shows at a glance items that are arranged in a logical order and which the researcher can check against.
- Interview – a conversation between a researcher and a respondent the purpose of which is to elicit information on a certain topic.
- Qualitative research – pertains to quality, aiming to gain insight through the study of individuals such as a lengthy individual interview or an in-depth case study.
- Quantitative research – pertains to quantity; aiming to study the relationship of one set of facts to another using scientific methods, e.g. a questionnaire sent to 1000 people.
- Questionnaire – a list or series of questions designed to elicit certain information.

Presentation of findings

Experiment with different ways of presenting your findings. Data taken from surveys and questionnaires need to be put into categories and groups so that the reader will be able to see patterns and extract significant information. Numerical data can be presented in many ways: tables, bar charts, histograms or graphs. These are the simplest methods of presenting your data; if you have access to a computer, then you may be able to produce very elaborate presentations. Photographs, video or audio recordings may also be used.

Below are examples of what a table, pie chart and histogram look like.

Table 1.2.6

	2002	**2006**	**2011**
under 5 years	273,610	300,246	337,240
5–12 years	431,350	450,720	487,782
13–18 years	361,420	340,367	329,742

Pie Chart

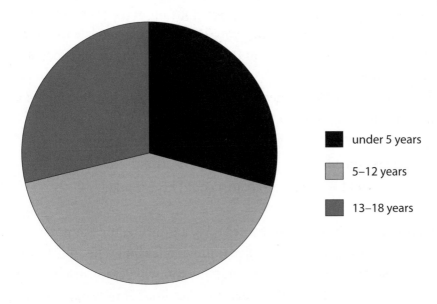

■	under 5 years
■	5–12 years
■	13–18 years

Histogram

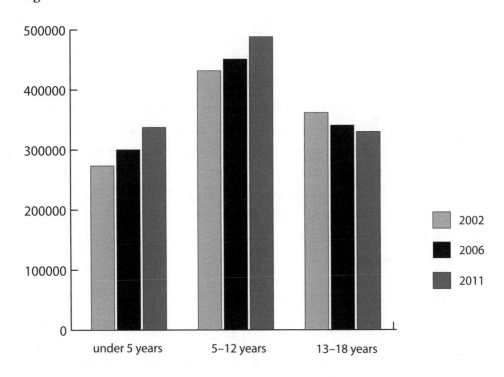

When you have presented your findings, it is important to describe what you have found, drawing attention to significant points, what surprised you and which results were predictable. How did your first-hand findings relate to the literature you read as secondary sources? For example, if you study a group of 15-year-olds playing computer games over a period of time, then you should be able to relate this to what is said in your text books about adolescent development on the one hand, and the effects of gaming on the other.

Be critical of yourself and your methodology and indicate improvements you could make if doing the project again.

- Were you surprised by anything you discovered while doing your project?
- Comment on bias and any ethical issues that have arisen.
- Suggest ways that you feel the research area could be extended.

In your evaluation do not be afraid to be negative, admitting, for example 'In my questionnaire, answers given to no. X revealed nothing relevant to the study because I had phrased the question badly.' By admitting this you will demonstrate that you have acquired an insight into the skill of devising questions. However, if you try to cover up or glance over the fact the some part of your research was not a success hoping that it will not be noticed, you will show that you have gained little in the way of skill – or that you are a dishonest researcher!

Appendices

In the appendix, include material not suitable for the main part of your study, for example newspaper cuttings, an observation, the questionnaire that you used, a copy of a table of statistics. Number them clearly, as the purpose of appendices is that you can refer to them in the main text.

Keep a record of all your planning notes. This is part of the research. Sometimes you will do a lot of background work, which will not be evident in your written submission, and it is recommended to provide evidence of all your project work, which can go in an appendix.

References and bibliography

An outline of the 'Harvard System' of referencing is given below. There are other systems and this is why you will notice that references and bibliographies may be presented differently in different books. All methods are broadly similar but whatever one you adopt you should stick to it or both you and your readers will be totally confused.

Referencing

In-text references are either quotations or citations.

- Quotations must be taken word for word from the original text.
- Short quotations begin and end with a single inverted comma.

  'Those mammals that have a period of adolescence seem to get through it much more quickly than humans' (Morgan, 2007.33)

- Longer quotations (three or more lines) are set out separately from the enclosing paragraph; they are usually indented and do not have quotation marks.

  Everything about globalisation is complex – how it is understood and its effects on all of us. The complexity of understandings, positions and debates that I have introduced in this chapter presents difficulties for a simple analysis… *(Forde et al, 2009.245)*

- If you do not quote a sentence in full you indicate this by use of an **ellipsis** (…) as in the example above.
- Please note in the example that the reference is placed in brackets at the end of the quote and consists of the authors' surnames and the year of publication, followed by the page number.

Citations

If the author's name is part of the sentence you should put the year of publication in brackets (parentheses).

Devlin (2012) argues that the youth work sector has been unusually active and positive in the areas of quality standards.

References

At the end of your project, essay or report you should list the references by author surname alphabetically.

For books:
Author's surname, followed by initials. Year of publication. *Title*. Place of publication: Publisher.

  Example: Santrock, J. W. (2011). *Adolescence* (14 ed.). London: McGraw-Hill.

For journal articles:

Author's surname, initials. Date of publication. '*Title of article.*' Name of journal Volume number Issue number: Pages.

> Example: O'Neill, C. 2010. '*Burn One Beacon, Light Many Fires.*' Youth Work Now, Winter 2010, p. 9. CDYSB.

For edited collections:

Surname of editor, Initials. Ed. Year of Publication. *Title.* Place: Publisher.

> Example: Forde, C., E. Kiely and R. Meade. Eds. 2009. *Youth and Community Work Perspectives.* Dublin: Blackhall Publishing.

To reference a chapter in edited collections:

> Example: Kehily, M.J., 2007. 'Education' in *Youth in Context: frameworks, settings and encounters.* Ed. M. Robb. London: Sage. Ch. 5.

Electronic sources:

Website Information: Author, Year, *Title*, Medium, Location URL, access or cited date in brackets. Note: it is important also to print out the first page as web pages change frequently or indeed may disappear altogether. You may put these pages in an appendix.

> Example: Anglia Ruskin University, 2012. *The Harvard System of Referencing.* (online).
>
> Available from: http://libweb.anglia.ac.uk/referencing/harvard.htm [Accessed on 16 June 2012]

DVD source: Author, Year. *Title*, Medium, Place: Publisher.

> Example: Evanescence, 2006. *Anywhere But Home.* (DVD) NYC, Sony Music Studios.

YouTube Video: Screen name of contributor, Year, *Video Title*, Series Title, Medium. Location URL, [Accessed: date].

> Example: Sir Ken Robinson, 2007. *Do Schools Kill Creativity?*, TEDTalks, video online. Available at *http://www.youtube.com/watch?v=iG9CE55wbtY* (accessed 20 June 2012).

For a PDF version of a government publication or similar publication.
Author, Year, *Title,* Medium. Place of Publication: Publisher. Location URL. [Accessed: date].

> Example: Department of Education and Science. 2003. (PDF) The National Youth Work Development Plan 2003-2007. Dublin: Government Stationery Office. *http://www.youth.ie/sites/youth.ie/files/nydp_03_07.pdf* [Accessed 22 May 2012]

Please note:

- The use of punctuation marks: commas, full stops, colons and quotations marks (the latter in relation to journal articles).
- Indentation of the second line of the reference so that the surname of the first author is easily identified.
- If there are more than three authors, the citation lists the first surname followed by 'et al' e.g. Dodge et al. 2002
- Second and subsequent authors' initials come before the surname.
- There are many finer points to be learned about referencing; only the basics are included here. Probably the best way to learn is to note how references are handled in your textbooks and other books that you will read.
- The Anglia Ruskin website URL *http://libweb.anglia.ac.uk/referencing/harvard.htm* (accessed 29 June 2012) has excellent and detailed guidelines on the complete Harvard system for any source imaginable that you might find – TV programmes, law reports, maps, blogs, podcasts and so on.

Glossary of terms

- Analysis – to analyse is to examine carefully for patterns and meanings.
- Bias – a slant or point of view. A study is said to be biased if the researcher has been subjective (let their own beliefs and assumptions overcome everything else) and influenced or prejudiced the outcome.
- Bibliography – a list of all books, articles, blogs and other sources that the researcher has read or consulted which have informed the author.
- Citation – a passage referred to or words quoted from the work of another author.
- Closed questions – have pre-set answers. The researcher limits the range of answers. (See also **questionnaire** and **open questions**) For example: do you smoke? Yes/No.

- Confidentiality – adherence to principles of trust and privacy; every individual has a right to privacy regarding information that is collected about them.

- Content analysis – an examination and classification of the subject matter of and approach taken by a document, media article or programme, book, letter or report in order to find patterns and information.

- Critical thinking – looking at the evidence and arguments for and against a topic and coming to a logical conclusion based on these.

- Data – facts, quantities or conditions that are given or known.

- Discuss – to debate, to argue the pros and cons.

- Evaluation – 'Is it worthwhile?' Overall, is it good/bad?

- Hypothesis – a theory; a speculation on what might be.

- Longitudinal survey – a study undertaken over a period of time; it could be weeks or years.

- Methodology – the research techniques used to collect information for the research project.

- Non-participant – no involvement with or influence on the subject.

- Objective – external to the researcher's own mind, feelings or values. This is the opposite of subjective. (Note: this word should not be confused with the 'objectives' of a project, which means how you will carry out the aim.)

- Official statistics – facts and figures contained in authorized public sources.

- Open question – allows the respondent to give a broad, informative and in-depth answer if they wish to do so. 'What do you think of...?' 'Could you tell me how you feel about....?'

- Opinion poll – a survey of people's opinions

- Participant – a member of the group being considered by the researcher

- Quotation – the use of an author's exact words.

- References – a list and description of all the works (e.g. books, articles, websites) which have either been quoted or mentioned in a text.

- Reliability – whether the research method used produce the same or similar results every time it is carried out in the same conditions.

- Representative sample – a section of the population that is typical of the general population. There is a specific formula to work this out.

- Respondent – a person who replies to questions or who allows himself to be interviewed.

- Response rate – the number or percentage of people who participate in the research.
- Sample – the numbers of people/groups about whom facts are gathered.
- Structured interviews – a very tightly organised interview with set questions.
- Subjective – relating to the researcher's own opinions, feelings and thoughts.
- Unstructured interview – an open interview in which the interviewer is given scope to rephrase questions or to ask extra ones.

References, resources and further reading

http://libweb.anglia.ac.uk/referencing/harvard.htm
www.fetac.ie

Index